ANXIETY AND WONDER

ANXIETY AND WONDER

On Being Human

MARIA BALASKA

BLOOMSBURY ACADEMIC
LONDON · NEW YORK · OXFORD · NEW DELHI · SYDNEY

BLOOMSBURY ACADEMIC
Bloomsbury Publishing Plc
50 Bedford Square, London, WC1B 3DP, UK
1385 Broadway, New York, NY 10018, USA
29 Earlsfort Terrace, Dublin 2, Ireland

BLOOMSBURY, BLOOMSBURY ACADEMIC and the Diana logo are
trademarks of Bloomsbury Publishing Plc

First published in Great Britain 2024

Copyright © Maria Balaska, 2024

Maria Balaska has asserted her right under the Copyright, Designs and
Patents Act, 1988, to be identified as Author of this work.

For legal purposes the Acknowledgements on pp. xi–xii constitute
an extension of this copyright page.

Cover image: *Flowers Made of Earth* (© Péris Iérémiadis)

A catalogue record for this book is available from the British Library.

A catalog record for this book is available from the Library of Congress.

ISBN: HB: 978-1-3503-0292-1
          PB: 978-1-3503-0293-8
          ePDF: 978-1-3503-0294-5
          eBook: 978-1-3503-0295-2

Typeset by Integra Software Services Pvt. Ltd.
Printed and bound in Great Britain

To find out more about our authors and books visit www.bloomsbury.com
and sign up for our newsletters.

Hast thou ever raised thy mind to the consideration of EXISTENCE, in and by itself, as the mere act of existing?

Hast thou ever said to thyself thoughtfully, IT IS! heedless, in that moment, whether it were a man before thee, or a flower, or a grain of sand? Without reference, in short, to this or that particular mode or form of existence? If thou hast, indeed, attained to this, thou wilt have felt the presence of a mystery, which must have fixed thy spirit in awe and wonder.

The very words, There is nothing! or, There was a time, when there was nothing! are self-contradictory. There is that within us which repels the proposition with as full and instantaneous light, as if it bore evidence against the fact in the right of its own eternity.

Not TO BE, then, is impossible: TO BE, incomprehensible. If thou hast mastered this intuition of absolute existence, thou wilt have learnt likewise, that it was this, and no other, which in the earlier ages seized the nobler minds, the elect among men, with a sort of sacred horror. This it was which first caused them to feel within themselves a something inevitably greater than their own individual nature.

Samuel Taylor Coleridge, The Friend.

To Paul
Στον Παύλο

CONTENTS

PREFACE

Centring a book around experiences can be challenging, particularly when these are unusual and difficult to understand. Then they can be treated as subjective and met with scepticism, or worse, with indifference.

The anxious wonder explored in this book may be rare, but what is even rarer is the attempt and capacity to understand it in the light of our existence, to recognize in it an insight about who we are and what we are for. Having the right conceptual framework for the experiences herein described can make them appear less alien and strange. This is not the only case where having the right framework for understanding a state of mind can allow for that state of mind to occur more regularly and can enable us to identify it. As we deepen our understanding of ourselves and the world, our emotional life and our awareness of it become more complex; this can sometimes manifest itself negatively in the disheartening phenomenon of individuals who, failing to mature their understanding alongside their age, exhibit the affective nuance of teenagers.

Making available to someone an experience that they have never had before is an impossible task. However, what is not impossible is creating conditions for attention. After all, it is well known to therapists and to those who have undergone therapy that a great deal of our mental life, the fleeting and the inconspicuous, becomes present to us only in the context of free-floating attention.

While writing this book, I decided that I did not want it to become a merely exegetical project. This decision aligns with an important theme in the book, that insofar as these experiences tell us something about the human existence, they connect us to ourselves as philosophical beings and to philosophy as a place where the human mind dwells by nature. Thus, I wanted to find a way to speak to this philosophical dwelling place in every reader, not just the professional philosopher. Further, given my background in psychoanalysis, a question arose for me whether there can be space for our philosophical nature within psychoanalysis or whether the transcendent dimension of our existence risks going unnoticed or unappreciated when we only associate our moods and emotions with worldly concerns. As a result, I wanted to write in a way that is also accessible to psychotherapists. For readers more interested in the exegetical aspects and the secondary literature, the endnotes are the appropriate place to look.

ACKNOWLEDGEMENTS

In 2019, I had the pleasure of attending some of Irad Kimhi's lectures on anxiety at the University of Chicago. These solidified my sense that something deeply significant and elusive takes place in anxiety. I am thankful to Irad Kimhi for those lectures and also for directing my attention to Lacan's work on anxiety.

I am indebted to Erin Plunkett and Rob Penney, my weekly companions in reading and discussing Heidegger's and Patočka's work over the course of three years. I am also grateful to Erin for our inspiring conversations about Kierkegaard. Conversations with Ben Ware and Dave Cerbone, as well as their invaluable comments on the manuscript at different stages of the project, were immensely helpful, and I am deeply grateful to both of them.

Kate Withy's excellent book on Heidegger and the uncanny was important for my work; I also thank her for her helpful comments and discussions on these topics. I must also extend my thanks to my former colleague Hugo Strandberg for his thoughtful and insightful comments on the manuscript, and to Sacha Golob for his feedback on my discussion on wonder in Heidegger.

Various parts of this work were presented on different occasions. I received valuable feedback and comments from the participants of the Philosophy of Education Society of Great Britain seminar at University College London, the Philosophy and Psychoanalysis London Group, the Wittgenstein workshop at the University of East Anglia, the 26th British Wittgenstein Society annual lecture, the philosophy department seminar at the University of Nottingham, the conference 'Too Mad to be True' at Ghent University, and the conference 'Saying Nothing to Say: Sense, Silence, and Impossible Texts in the Twentieth Century' at the University of Warwick.

I am thankful to Liza Thompson at Bloomsbury for commissioning the book, and to Ben Piggott who took over and successfully saw this project through.

Constantine Sandis helped initiate this project and I am grateful for his friendly encouragement.

The writing of the book would not have been possible without the continuous support of my parents, Giorgos and Olympia, my sister, Amalia, as well as my friend Amy Tai.

The book is dedicated to my partner, Paul, with love.

London

August 2023

ABBREVIATIONS

Martin Heidegger:

B&T   *Being and Time*, trans. J. Macquarrie and E. Robinson. New York: Harper & Row, 1962.

WIM   'What Is Metaphysics?'. In *Basic Writings*, ed. and trans. D.F. Krell. London: Routledge, 2011.

Sigmund Freud:

SE   *The Standard Edition of the Complete Psychological Works of Sigmund Freud*, ed. and trans. James Strachey, 24 Volumes. London: Hogarth Press, 1973.

1
Introduction

1.1 Encounters with nothing

We sometimes find ourselves enveloped by overpowering moods[1] that are indefinite, devoid of any discernible object or direction. In these moods, we might, for example, suddenly feel like a weight is pressing down on us, or, conversely, like a burden has been lifted and every problem solved, even though when we attempt to understand the source of such intense affects, we find that no particular thing is weighing on us and no particular problem has been solved; our lives have not changed in any perceptible way but continue to house the same concerns and sources of joy. Yet, something moves us deeply and shakes us out of our usual states of mind. Such sudden and momentary shifts of mood without any discernible cause can seize us unexpectedly amidst mundane tasks, as we are driving, washing the dishes, getting dressed.[2] Similar to cases of déjà vu, it feels impossible to know whether the source of the experience is imagined or real, even though the experience itself is undoubtedly powerful.

In this book, I will treat these cases of being thrown out of our everyday existence as cases in which we are thrown into the question of existence, in which who we are and what we are for emerges as a question. In the history of philosophy, we find different names for such moods of existence, some with positive and other with negative affective overtones. Anxiety, wonder, awe, boredom, nausea are some of them. These terms should not be regarded as definitive or exhaustive portrayals of these moods: instead, they serve as umbrella terms that capture the tone of the experience, sufficiently complex to accommodate variations depending on who experiences them, when and where, and how prepared they are for them. In this book I will look mainly at philosophical descriptions of anxiety and wonder, although, as I discuss later, in some ways it may be more appropriate to speak of an anxious wonder. Even though at first sight anxiety and wonder seem to be opposing moods, within this context[3] anxiety and wonder draw closer and exhibit resemblances.

I am, then, interested more specifically in two kinds of cases: cases where the suspension of our ordinary lives assumes the form of an anxious malaise – an overwhelming sense that suddenly we do not know how to carry on with our lives, that something feels wrong or unfamiliar – and cases where this suspension takes a wondrous form, as if something very obvious about life suddenly became illuminated, leaving us with contentment. Again, it would be wrong to classify such moments as solely negative or positive; anxiety and wonder share both the unsettling sense that the flow of one's life is suspended for no apparent reason and the more joyous sense that we have access to something bigger, beyond our everyday lives. Feelings of insecurity and malaise can be found within the wonder, as can feelings of peace and joy within anxiety. This is why when we experience these moments in their full complexity we can speak of an anxious wonder.

That such affective experiences have no particular object or cause, does not mean that there is a specific object but we cannot identify it yet. Unawareness of the cause does not necessarily mean that there is no object. For example, sometimes, we are unclear about what we are affected by, but this may be because there are multiple objects causing our affective state, or because there is an object we do not really want to consider. In such cases, talking to a friend or a psychotherapist can help us find the source or sources of the mood. But in the cases I examine 'entities within the world are not relevant at all',[4] not even as a totality, when taken together. Rather, here one feels affected by *everything and nothing in particular*. By 'everything' I do not mean an exhaustive list of all the entities in one's life – one's marriage, job, children, etc. This would take us back to the case of a mood that is directed to multiple entities.

Because we cannot link such intense feelings to any particular entity in our world, once the mood dissipates, we often dismiss the uncanny sensation, by reassuring ourselves that 'it was really nothing'. We carry on with our lives as if nothing had ever happened. If so, if these episodes come and go away, like fragmentary recollections from our dreams, why choose to examine them? Why should we direct our attention towards these inconspicuous, fleeting moments, these encounters with nothing?

1.2 Learning from our moods

That it is worth attending to our moods as a means of gaining self-knowledge is not hard to comprehend. Feeling excitement at the prospect of seeing someone may reveal an underlying love for that person. Feeling anxious as one's fiftieth birthday approaches may reveal that one's life choices do not reflect what they had aspired to. A sense of boredom during a date may indicate an incompatibility between oneself and the other person. In such instances, the mood has a definite object and reveals something about that object. If we pose the question, 'What brings about my mood?' we can give answers like 'this person and my affection for them', 'my life trajectory thus far' or 'spending time with this individual'. Relatedly, the mood invites us to act in a certain way vis-à-vis the object(s) that elicited it in the first place. For instance, in the first case, we can acknowledge and express our feelings; in the second, we can initiate transformative changes or reconsider our life choices; in the third, we can discontinue the romantic involvement. In these ordinary cases of being affected by entities – be they things, situations or people within our worlds – the revelations offered by these moods concern the entities involved.

Such cases of learning from our moods align with the structure of our everyday existence. Most of the time we are affected by specific entities, which reflects a basic condition of our existence – what Martin Heidegger refers to as 'being in the midst of entities'. Daily activities like brushing our teeth, checking our smartphone, embracing our loved ones, cooking, daydreaming, meeting friends, working, eating, watching a film, listening to music or reading a newspaper exemplify the simple ways in which we find ourselves amidst entities (toothbrushes, phones, others, food, dreams, films, news, etc.). This does not mean that we never encounter the absence of entities. Indeed, within our everyday lives and involvements, we also encounter entities in their absence; we encounter entities *as* absent. The entities and activities we are engaged with in our everyday life can break down, disappear, come to an end. People die, relationships end, jobs are lost, tools break down. But such cases of absence still fall within the habitual mode I have described.

An entity that is absent, damaged or destroyed remains an entity (present in its absence).[5]

The idea that we are always in the midst of entities – even when an entity is absent – is not a description that depends on how each of us lives their life, whether one is surrounded by many entities or engages in many activities. Instead, it is a logical point about how human life is structured and how the world appears to us: even if one decides to isolate oneself from others and to refrain from any activities, our habitual way of being-in-the-world – how we act, speak and think – is through our relation to other entities. *Most of the time* we make sense of our emotions, moods and feelings by taking them to concern something specific and to ask what causes them.

But in today's *zeitgeist* this basic mode of how our human lives are structured is often taken to be the *only* mode available. The emotional life is exhaustively understood as a response to other entities, exemplified by traditional psychology's treatment of emotions in terms of natural causality and its adherence to a biological framework that views our emotional life in the light of evolutionary processes. From worry and fear to love and joy, emotions are explained in relation to our survival instincts, and, as I discuss later, objectless anxiety has been perceived as an evolutionary maladaptation of fear, inexpedient insofar as it does not increase our chances for survival. From this prevailing perspective, to be affected by a mood means to react to a specific object that is in principle determinable, with our own existence often being perceived as just another entity within the world.

If we accept uncritically that we are solely affected by other entities, then we have no way to explain these indefinite moods and what we can learn from them. It is precisely for this reason that philosophy should assume a role in our attempt to understand our emotional life. In fact, as I discuss later, philosophy itself originates in such strange, overpowering encounters with nothing.

1.3 Meaningfulness and possibility

So, what do we encounter when we are hit by such seeming objectless moods? The Czech philosopher Jan Patočka offers a description of such wonder:

> [There] are experiences that show something like the peculiarity, the strange wonderment of our situation – that *we are* at all and that *the world is,* that this is not self-evident, that there is something like an astonishing wonder, that things *appear* to us and that we ourselves are among them. [...] When I wonder in this way – it is strange, isn't it? Materially the world is completely the same as before, there are the same things, the same surroundings, the same chairs and tables, people and stars, and nevertheless there is something here *completely*

changed. No *new* thing has been discovered, no new reality; what has been discovered is not a *thing*, not a reality, but the fact that this everything *is*. But this 'everything *is*' is not a thing.[6]

It turns out that we do encounter something in these strange experiences, but this something has a different character compared to the objects of our ordinary experiences. In the ordinary cases, we are always affected by *something*, even when this something is unclear and vague, or consists of multiple things taken together. But here the object of these experiences, from a certain perspective, appears as a *nothing*. Instead of learning something about *this* or *that* in our lives, we learn that 'we are', 'the world is', 'everything is'. But the fact that we are and that the world is do not seem to offer any new knowledge and from a certain viewpoint they can seem empty, even tautological. We may be tempted to interpret this as a wonder at the material existence of the world – how arbitrary it is that life came to be, that Homo Sapiens evolved, that matter came into existence. Indeed, such realizations also sometimes evoke awe and even a sense of unease, a feeling of our smallness or insignificance in the grand scheme of life. However, these facts about life in the universe would hardly deserve to be called 'not a thing, not a reality'. They are fascinating discoveries, the outcomes of epistemic progress throughout the ages. Instead, here we are concerned with something related but distinct. We learn what we already knew but had not realized its significance: that we are in a world, and that things are intelligible within our being-in-the-world (they *appear* to us).[7] That we are in the world and that things appear to us are two ways to describe the same thing: that we can make sense of things. But why does the simple fact that we are in a world and that we are sense makers deserve wonder, or anxiety?

Sense-making is as mysterious as it is ordinary. On the one hand, the fact that things make sense to us is an inherent aspect of the human condition, our lives are saturated with meaning and sense, and, in that sense, we make sense of things all the time. On the other hand, insofar as things make sense to us, we are called to make sense of things; the fact that sense is given does not mean that all we can do is passively drift along in various contexts of meaning. Instead, we possess the capacity to place things in meaning, to open new worlds and make things present by making sense of them. Why we have this capacity and how it emerged, we do not know. Taking it for granted, we often neglect it, carried along by contexts of meaning that we have inherited without much involvement. But moods like anxiety and wonder can be passionate reminders of the fact that we are active participants in sense-making. What we encounter in such moods are not just abstract conditions for meaning but ourselves as potential cases of 'enworldling and contextualizing [...] within a set of possibilities that makes things able to be known and used in terms of those very possibilities'.[8]

To form worlds means to open contexts of meaning and, thereby, to open possibilities of being-in-the-world. Worlds are contexts and structures within which things make sense. A thing appears to us as a skillet in the world of a kitchen: we make sense of it through the context of the practice in which we use it (in this case, cooking). A piece of paper can appear to us as a work of art in a museum exhibition. A total stranger can appear to us as a fellow creature of God in the context of a religious practice, and so on. When we are in therapy, part of the process entails thinking about ourselves and others in a different light, opening new contexts of meaning: this can transform our relation to ourselves and others. The specific worlds within which things become present in a specific way – such as the world of a kitchen or a museum or a church – are a manifestation of the fact that we can form worlds in the first place, that we are always in the context of a world, that things can appear as meaningful to us.[9] This is what comes forth in these experiences, sometimes creating a sense of anxious wonder. We see that we are cases of world-forming, open to possibility, a taste of our existential freedom.[10] As I discuss throughout the book, this basic capacity to form worlds is closely related to existential freedom and possibility.

Patočka believes that experiencing this strange fact, that things are meaningful to us, links to the human capacity for spiritual existence, and can open up a 'new manner of life'. Learning from these experiences can allow us to change and deepen our lives, to see them in the light of possibility, precisely because they can partake into a meaningful world. This does not mean to see them in the light of 'anything is possible', and it is not about being free to be however we want to be or do whatever we want.[11] A life-in-possibility does not just mean a life of 'free-floating potentiality', a 'liberty of indifference'.[12] Rather, in anxiety and wonder, possibility emerges not only as a given, but also as a task and responsibility. This is why the question of sin is discussed in Chapter 4: human existence can – and indeed structurally does – fail to live up to possibility due to its ambivalence towards it; it loves and flees from possibility simultaneously.[13]

This seemingly empty but crucial insight about human existence renders these strange and uncanny moments worthy of our attention. This insight is not restricted to particulars of one's life, but addresses more generally the question of what is possible for the individual insofar as they partake into human existence. Because, in this case, one learns about oneself as a case of human existence, I will sometimes refer to it as an ontological insight.

1.4 Structure of the book

To tell a story about how these strange moods give us an ontological insight, and thereby allow us to enrich our lives, I draw upon themes from the works of Martin Heidegger and

Søren Kierkegaard on anxiety and on wonder. Other voices also appear in the book, including Plato, Patočka, Arendt, Wittgenstein, Freud and Lacan.

Chapters 2 and 3 focus on anxiety. The concept of anxiety has a distinctive place in our modern lives: it has become a core category in psychiatric diagnostic manuals, like the Diagnostic and Statistical Manual of Mental Disorders (DSM), and it is diagnosed in a very high number of cases worldwide. Treating anxiety is a frequently promised outcome of a variety of products and services, from vitamins and LED masks to buying a pet and going on yoga retreats. This distinctive feature of anxiety poses a unique challenge for the account that Heidegger and Kierkegaard present: can their account contribute to this situation or, is it restricted to understanding a niche, idiosyncratic phenomenon, given that they speak of objectless forms of anxiety? Yet, the feature of objectlessness has not escaped the attention of theories of psychopathology.[14] To explore this, I look at psychoanalysis, particularly the views of Sigmund Freud and Jacques Lacan. While they both acknowledge the challenge posed by the feature of objectlessness, they lack the necessary conceptual framework to fully comprehend it. Freud's account is constrained by his Darwinian interpretation of human existence, while Lacan's account remains confined within a perspective that cannot transcend finitude and groundlessness. In Chapter 2, I compare their accounts of anxiety with Heidegger's: what they overlook is the transcendent dimension of the human existence, a capacity to go beyond the actual and worldly concerns of our existence.

One cannot fully understand the emotional life of the human being, including episodes of anxiety, unless one takes into account that what it means to be human is an open question. This is why Kierkegaard thinks that psychology is inadequate for understanding anxiety.[15] As I further discuss in Chapter 3, bringing together Plato (Socrates) and Kierkegaard, to understand the complexities of our affective life, one needs to begin from the fact that the human condition is an enigma, that there is no clear direction about what the human being is and how it is meant to live its life. Kierkegaard draws our attention to the myth of Genesis, to tell a story about who we are. In that story anxiety emerges as a central element of our origin. The human being originates in a structural ambivalence towards the fact that it has access to what is possible, beyond what is actual.

This is yet another intriguing overlap between anxiety and wonder: in the history of ideas both moods have been linked to the theme of origins. The mood of anxiety figures in the myth of the original sin, and wonder has been characterized as the origin of philosophy. Chapter 4 looks into this link between wonder and philosophy, weaving together philosophical threads from Plato, Heidegger and Arendt. What does it mean that we are philosophical beings insofar as we wonder in this strange, objectless way and why do such uncanny moments open us onto philosophizing?

Chapter 5 looks at one more description of objectless wonder, Ludwig Wittgenstein's wonder at the fact that anything is. Wittgenstein's discussion introduces a new angle through his concern about the paradoxicality of these experiences: does the paradoxical nature of such encounters betray that they are nothing but linguistic illusions, cases of being entangled and led astray by our grammar? I dismiss the Wittgensteinian worry by showing why it is not a real concern for either Heidegger or Kierkegaard.

Finally, in Chapter 6, I explore the aftermath of being exposed to such strange experiences. What does life look like after anxiety and wonder, if we pay attention to them and learn from their insights? How does the fact that the world is intelligible and meaningful to us link to a potential for enriching our lives?

1.5 Kierkegaard and Heidegger

Kierkegaard is the first philosopher to tell a story about wonder and anxiety as instances of self-knowledge, and more specifically of knowledge of our openness to possibility. He is also the first to distinguish anxiety from fear on the basis of the status of their object: fear has an object, whereas anxiety's object is *nothing*.

Heidegger's account is directly influenced by Kierkegaard, 'the man who has gone farthest in analysing the phenomenon of anxiety'.[16] The two philosophers have their own terms about the object of these strange moods, with some terms being more challenging than others, like in Kierkegaard's work 'the possibility of being able', or 'spirit', and in Heidegger's work 'Being', 'the world as a whole', 'the whole as the whole'.[17]

Despite the differences in their philosophical vocabulary, I take them to agree on the following fundamental points. What emerges in these strange moods is the wondrous fact that things make sense to us in the first place, and that to the extent that we exercise the capacity for sense-making, human life is a life of possibility. In other words, the human life is linked to possibility thanks to our capacity to form worlds, to open possibilities of meaning. Further, they both recognize our constitutional ambivalence towards possibility and its existential freedom, hence the wonder at this capacity is an anxious one.

In suggesting that in these encounters with nothing we encounter ourselves as sense-makers, both Heidegger and Kierkegaard promote a dynamic view of the human existence. We are 'world-forming',[18] 'events of opening',[19] 'ongoing exercises of making intelligible',[20] cases of 'synthesis of psyche and body, [...] of the temporal and the eternal'.[21] We are those movements, insofar as we make them or embody them. This view is as valuable as it is rare. A dynamic picture of the human existence as a doing or a happening is very different from the various static perspectives that we are used to employing when we think about ourselves. To give some examples of static views of the human existence, we usually think of the human as an evolved organism, or as a psychological subject (a subject of experiences), or as a subject of language, or as a creature in the image of God. Sometimes, or most of the times, we think of ourselves as a combination of such pictures. In such cases, who we are is already decided, and no matter what we do, we can always rely on these descriptions to define ourselves. Whereas it is a fascinating common thread between Heidegger and Kierkegaard that being human is an open question, addressed and sustained in what we do, in exercising the capacity to make sense of ourselves and the world.

One crucial challenge when bringing Heidegger and Kierkegaard together concerns Kierkegaard's Christian background and theological assumptions, raising the question of how much of that Heidegger shares. In my discussion, I refrain from using theological terms, where possible. For example, I discuss Kierkegaard's 'wonder' and 'paradox' in relation to the eruption of possibility in general, rather than Christ's incarnation as a particular and narrow historical expression of the former. However, I do explore Kierkegaard's concept of 'anxiety' in connection to the myth of the Fall and the archetype of Adam. The complex nature and degree of theological undertones in these two philosophers, as well as the significance of their differences in this regard, are not explicitly addressed in this discussion. However, it is worth considering two points.[22]

First, what Heidegger treats as the problem with ontotheology is its 'system of dogma'[23] and its attempt to get rid of the nothing by grounding existence in God. But despite the heavily Christian undertones in Kierkegaard's treatment of the topic, his account resists Heidegger's main criticism of ontotheology.[24] Traditionally God is seen as what offers a source of necessity against the contingency of existence and plays a grounding role against the nothing, that is, God's existence is *why* there is something rather than nothing. If the principal worry, then, is that ontotheology attempts to eliminate the nothing, the extent to which Kierkegaard's work deserves that worry is not at all clear. Because, although it is undeniably true that, for Kierkegaard, human existence cannot be disconnected from our attraction to and longing for the divine, God does not play a grounding role in his work. For example, one of Kierkegaard's points in the two texts I focus on – *The Concept of Anxiety* (where he writes using the pseudonym Vigilius Haufniensis) and *Philosophical Fragments* (where he writes using the pseudonym Johannes Climacus[25]) – is that our coming-into-existence did not arise out of necessity, has no logical or other ground, but has, instead, a dimension of wondrous mystery. Further, by placing anxiety at the heart of our origin and by describing it as something that can never be fully overcome,[26] Kierkegaard's work undoubtedly holds a central place for the nothing.

Second, Heidegger's own work is not entirely cut off from theological concepts, and a tension persists throughout his writings. As I hinted earlier, Heidegger's account of human existence includes concepts that originate from a theological context (such as 'falling', 'guilt', 'conscience'). This is not a case of 'an obvious contradiction, or a piece of self-serving disingenuousness',[27] but it is Heidegger's way of reclaiming these concepts while at the same time avoiding a disavowal of what can be deep and original in theological thinking.[28] It is an open question whether he succeeds in doing so, especially, when Kierkegaard's account of anxiety, which directly influenced Heidegger, is intimately connected to the myth of the Fall. But I take this open question to be a fruitful basis for exploration.

2

What makes us anxious?

2.1 Dysfunction or potential?

There are two dominant narratives regarding anxiety, which Gerrit Glas summarizes as follows: 'the medical literature, in which anxiety is described as a dysfunctional alarm response that is elicited by biological, cognitive, and learning mechanisms' and 'a large, older, body of literature that describes anxiety as an existential phenomenon, expressing the meaning of universal facts of life such as, for instance, the threat of absurdity, isolation, and/or imminent non – being.'[1] These two accounts can coexist without significantly influencing each other, as they operate within their respective domains. The medical perspective focuses on psychopathology, treats anxiety as dysfunction or disorder and offers solutions such as medication, therapy and relaxation techniques. Meanwhile, the existential perspective on anxiety is associated with the recognition of finitude, often manifesting itself during a mid-life crisis or moments of existential reflection. If existential anxiety becomes overwhelming and debilitating, then it is considered a case of psychopathology that requires intervention.

With the account of anxiety that I present here I aim to deepen the existential perspective in a way that challenges some of the assumptions of the medical, psychopathological perspective. Although it should be acknowledged that anxiety can, in some cases, be debilitating and in need of treatment, one cannot understand what qualifies as a symptom or a disorder, without considering what it means for a human to function well or fulfill its purpose. To give a somewhat simplistic example, if one thinks that a state of constant 'highs' is possible or even desirable for human life, then one is bound to see the 'lows' as a dysfunction that requires treatment. Taking seriously the idea that powerful and disturbing moods can also arise in response to our existence and its tasks can change how we view anxiety. Kierkegaard, for example, interprets the anxiety of the hypochondriac and the anxiety of children as manifestations of the human openness to possibility,[2] rather than restricting his account to idiosyncratic existential moments experienced by 'mentally healthy' adults. To deepen the existential perspective on anxiety, I will focus on what I take to be the decisive feature of such experiences, their objectlessness.

It is because they focus on the nature of the object of such experiences that neither Kierkegaard nor Heidegger offers any detailed or definite description of what anxiety feels like. They both distinguish anxiety from fear and common anxiousness,[3] but the distinction is drawn on the basis of the kind of object involved. Fear and anxiety are 'kindred phenomena,'[4] affective siblings, but whereas in fear (and phobias) we fear specific things, such as spiders, flying, water, heights, etc., in anxiety the threat is indefinite.

As suggested in the previous chapter, the term 'anxiety' offers a general direction of what this experience feels like, but it is not the only nor the final term used. For example, Kierkegaard describes anxiety as an experience of dizziness, while Heidegger's descriptions of anxiety often resemble panic, depression, depersonalization, or derealization. To mention only some of his descriptions, in anxiety one feels uncanny, all things and we ourselves sink into indifference; beings slip away, we slip away from ourselves; anxiety is an unsettling experience of hovering where there is nothing to hold on to, a malaise related to a vacant stillness.[5] Other descriptions offered may sound odd as they point away from what we ordinarily qualify as a negative experience and towards what we ordinarily qualify as a positive experience. Kierkegaard speaks of a pleasant anxiousness, but also of anxiety as something we love[6] and Heidegger connects it to a strange kind of calm.[7] They both suggest that being prepared for anxiety allows us to experience it as something to be grateful for, involving, as Heidegger says, 'cheerfulness and gentleness'.[8]

Such descriptions, or even the lack thereof, may be seen as a failure to converse with psychology and psychiatry.[9] Yet it should be first acknowledged that the differences between the psychopathology story and the story I present here run much deeper than a mere difference in the description of what the experience feels like. The way we experience and describe anxiety depends on our assumptions about the nature of human existence, and for Heidegger and Kierkegaard anxiety reveals a dimension of human existence that is entirely absent from the way psychology and psychiatry understand the human being.

One of the predominant and largely unquestioned ideas that permeates the familiar mental health discourse is the view that anxiety is always (part of) a mental disorder, a dysfunction that manifests through various symptoms. Phobias, panic disorders, separation anxiety disorders, generalized anxiety disorder are some of the disorders that qualify as an anxiety disorder. To know, however, what qualifies as dysfunction, one must have an idea of what it means for a being to function well, and what it means for a being to function well will depend on how one understands that being in the first place. In all scientific research traditions that offer an account of anxiety – ethological, behaviourist and cognitive – our affective life is treated within the distinction between the natural and the environmental and they are seen as a dysfunction when they do not help us adapt well.[10] Hence, as I discuss below, the only way such models can explain objectless anxiety is through the idea of evolutionary maladaptation. But although our animality and sociality are undoubtedly valid descriptions of the human, such descriptions have no space for the dimension I discuss in this book, namely, that we are open to possibility.

In contrast, having an entirely different starting point in response to the question about human existence, both Kierkegaard and Heidegger take a critical distance from the priority of what anxiety 'feels like'. Relatedly, their accounts also take a critical distance from the usual distinction between positive and negative feelings that is so central for the psychopathological interpretation of anxiety. In the psychopathology story, anxiety must be treated precisely because of its negative affective quality and its negative impact on the individual's life. But Kierkegaard challenges the simplistic distinction between what causes feelings of antipathy and what causes feelings of sympathy, when he describes anxiety as 'an antipathetic sympathy or a sympathetic antipathy', an 'ambivalent state' that is generated 'by the lure of possibility'.[11] Here the starting point is not what anxiety feels like; what it feels like – its ambivalent nature – emerges from the inherent elusiveness of its object, namely, possibility. Heidegger, too, has been critical of the prioritization of subjective experience (what it feels like) and the reduction of anxiety to observable and classifiable negative feelings[12]:

[I]f we dissociate anxiety […] from its relation to the nothing; then we are left with anxiety as an isolated 'feeling' that can be distinguished from other feelings and dissected amid a familiar assortment of psychic states observed by psychology. Along the guidelines of a facile distinction between 'higher' and 'lower' these 'moods' can then be classified as either uplifting or depressing. The zealous pursuit of 'types' and 'countertypes' of 'feelings' and of varieties and subspecies of these 'types' will never run out of prey.[13]

So, the phenomenon that Kierkegaard and Heidegger describe cannot be properly understood unless one identifies and avoids certain misconceptions about the human life of the mind, misconceptions that characterize the psychopathology perspective on anxiety. Instead, for them, the right starting point for their enquiry into certain forms of anxiety is that they are objectless, or as they put it, that their object is 'something that is nothing'.[14,15] By 'nothing' they do not mean a complete absence of entities. If this were the case, then it would be an encounter with something, albeit something absent. Because at the level of entities there is no change, no absent or broken entity that could explain a sense of absence or withdrawal, what is withdrawn must be something that is not an entity. As I suggested in the first chapter, this is the simple, background condition of meaningfulness, that the world is and that we are at all. This is most of the times unnoticed, taken for granted in a way that backgrounds our everyday dealings with entities. But in anxiety it withdraws and becomes present through its absence: 'something that is a nothing'.

It is important to remark that anxiety's difference from fear on the basis of a lack of object also occurs as a description within the psychopathology discourse.[16] This means that, through the descriptions of its 'patients', the psychopathology perspective may also often deal with objectless forms of anxiety. In fact, as I am about to discuss, for some thinkers in that tradition, the objectlessness is not just a marginal case, but an essential feature of the phenomenon of anxiety. But, as I discuss, the psychopathology discourse is generally ill-equipped to understand the objectlessness, and the related distinction between anxiety and fear.

To explore the challenges of understanding anxiety's objectlessness, I turn my attention to Sigmund Freud. Freud interests me because of a palpable tension in his writings around anxiety. He also interests me because Jacques Lacan, follower of Freud and psychoanalyst, attempts to integrate his psychoanalytic account of anxiety with the existentialist perspective. Both Freud and Lacan seem to recognize in anxiety's objectlessness more than a narrow category of the phenomenon. Instead, they seem to think that understanding the nature of its distinction from fear (on the basis of a lack of specific object) is significant for understanding the phenomenon of anxiety in general. Nevertheless, as I discuss, their respective accounts of human existence fall short in capturing the essence of this lack of specific object.

In what follows, I examine three interpretations of the feature of objectlessness. First, Freud's account views anxiety's lack of a specific object as a result of evolutionary maladaptation. Second, Lacan's account relates anxiety to the groundlessness of our life projects and to desire as inherently driven by lack. Finally, Heidegger's account regards the absence of a specific object as a characteristic of what comes forth in objectless anxiety, namely the givenness of meaning. Through this progression from Freud to Lacan[17] and then to Heidegger, a narrative unfolds that moves from viewing anxiety as an organism's maladaptive response to perceiving it as a signal of the finitude of human desire, and, finally, to understanding anxiety as indicating more than finitude, namely, our openness to possibility.[18]

2.2 The 'riddle' of anxiety in Freud

Freud is aware that the phenomenon of anxiety poses a challenge to the biological, phylogenetic and physiological explanations that seem more appropriate for fear. He refers to anxiety as a riddle: 'the problem of anxiety is a nodal point at which the most various and important questions converge, a riddle whose solution would be bound to throw a flood of light on our whole mental existence'.[19]

Freud tries out various ideas about the function of anxiety, considering it first as a result of accumulated excitation that has not been adequately discharged, then a transformation of libido and, finally, as a signal of a threatening traumatic situation or danger, an exogenous or endogenous threat. Anxiety serves as a signal in situations of helplessness and impending danger, where we anticipate the trauma and behave as if it has already occurred. The kinds of dangerous situations that Freud has in mind vary, often depending on the particular period of life or developmental phase of the individual, but they revolve around loss or separation, such as the loss of love, an object loss, castration.[20] These are all versions of the primal source of anxiety, the separation from the mother.[21] Whereas Freud initially held the view, later expressed by Otto Rank, that birth is the primal source of anxiety,[22] later he distanced himself from it.[23] Other mammals are also born, Freud notices, yet this fact does not cause anxiety attacks in them.[24,25]

Despite Freud's distinction between the ego and the animal organism, when it comes to the reasons why humans are so prone to being traumatized by loss and to anxiety as an anticipation of a repetition of loss, Freud also lists biological and phylogenetic factors along with psychological factors. The biological factor is our short intrauterine existence: it means that we are more helpless and in need of a caring figure when we are born. The phylogenetic factor is a strange fact about our sexual development, namely, that our sexual life, unlike that of most of the animals nearly related to us, 'does not make a steady advance from birth to maturity, but undergoes a very decided interruption'[26] around the fifth year. This, for Freud, means that 'the majority of the instinctual demands of this infantile sexuality are treated by the ego as dangers and fended off',[27] causing anxiety. Finally, there is the psychological factor, the distinction and simultaneous presence of the ego and the id that make us more prone to internal dangers to which we respond with anxiety. As Freud puts it, 'in view of the dangers of [external] reality, the ego is obliged to guard against certain instinctual impulses in the id and to treat them as dangers',[28] but because the ego is 'intimately bound up with the id', it can only 'fend off an instinctual danger by restricting its own organization and by acquiescing in the formation of symptoms in exchange for having impaired the instinct'.[29] In other words, contrary to the case where I perceive a threat and I respond by fight or flight, when the threat is internal, the ego has to sacrifice a part of its own self.

The last-mentioned point is one of the reasons why anxiety is, as Freud characterizes it, 'inexpedient'. Contrary to those cases when the danger is external and the entity in danger can flee from that danger when it gets a signal, here the response to an internal danger means that the entity has to flee from itself, as it were. Freud also frames the inexpedient character of anxiety through its distinction from fear, although he does not acknowledge the philosophical roots of that distinction:

The affect of anxiety exhibits one or two features the study of which promises to throw further light on the subject. Anxiety [angst] has an unmistakable relation to expectation, it is anxiety about something. It has a quality of indefiniteness and lack of object. In precise speech we use the word fear [*Furcht*] rather than anxiety [*Angst*] if it has found an object. Real danger is a danger that is known, and realistic anxiety is anxiety about a known danger of this sort. Neurotic anxiety is anxiety about an unknown danger. Neurotic danger is thus a danger that has still to be discovered. By bringing this danger which is not known to the ego into consciousness the analyst makes neurotic anxiety no different from realistic anxiety so that it can be dealt with in the same way.[30]

Freud suggests that anxiety is a disorder insofar as it lacks an object; thus, the goal of treatment would be to transform anxiety into fear by finding its object. According to the above passage, realistic anxiety would essentially be another term for fear, while neurotic anxiety would be the appropriate term for anxiety.[31] Yet the gap between fear and anxiety widens even further when Freud realizes that even what he calls, in the above passage, 'realistic anxiety' is in some sense unrealistic: 'on further consideration we must tell ourselves that our judgment that realistic anxiety is rational and expedient calls for a drastic revision'.[32] Freud juxtaposes signal anxiety to the case of a frightened animal where the signal for danger is more appropriately linked to fear, as it connects to an object, fear of the predator, of being eaten, etc.: 'A terrified animal is afraid and flees; but the expedient part in this is the flight not the being afraid. [...] Thus one feels tempted to conclude that anxiety is *never* an expedient thing'.[33]

Notice the tension between the human and the animal. Freud's mention of the danger signal in the animal world is crucial, for it highlights the idea that an affect functions well when it serves the purpose of self-preservation. Indeed, Freud acknowledges his debt to Darwin and the idea that emotions are connected to actions that originally served a purpose.[34] This physiological model of the affective life entails the assumption that adaptation is a fundamental function of the human being[35]: the capacity to foresee a traumatic situation links to the instinct for self-preservation. From this perspective, the human is shaped by a tension between its animal nature (Homo Sapiens) and the socio-cultural environment it inhabits.[36] If affects are, as Samuel Arbiser suggests Freud believed, 'hysterias of the species', then anxiety is a maladaptive affect, which had an original function as fear, but no longer fulfils that function. This can be likened to the innate ability of a human baby to swim, which is lost after a few weeks of extra-uterine life.[37]

If we take the expedience of an affect to be directly related to how adaptive it makes us, and we think that humans, like other animals, adapt to difficulties governed by an aim of survival in the face of threats, then anxiety can only be viewed as a malfunction.[38] Lacan picks up on the reductivism that this view involves and remedies it by shifting the focus from the ego as an evolved organism to the human as a speaking subject.[39]

2.3 Lacan and the anxiety in front of a mirror

Lacan presents his most systematic account of anxiety in the seminar dedicated to the subject, Seminar X. There he brings together various descriptions of anxiety, including Kierkegaard's own,[40] and avoids treating these as distinct types of anxiety. The feature of objectlessness is, for him, pivotal in understanding this multidimensional phenomenon. Unlike Freud, who is puzzled by anxiety's lack of object and views it as a malfunctioning affect, Lacan regards the objectlessness as the key to understanding anxiety and offers his own unique reading of it.

To analyse anxiety, Lacan offers a remarkably mundane example. Whereas our gaze in the mirror typically feels familiar, sometimes we may catch a glimpse of our own gaze and feel a momentary sense of threat, as if we were being looked at by a stranger: we feel anxious. This experience can resemble depersonalization but it need not be associated with the condition of depersonalization, as it can occur as an isolated experience, without additional symptoms. Remarkably, even an extended period of contemplation of our mirror image can, if we remain attuned to the experience, engender unease and an anxious anticipation of impending danger.

By employing such an ordinary example, but also one that links to the domain of the mirror, which Lacan associates more generally with the emergence of human subjectivity, he takes a different approach from Freud. Here is Lacan's description of this moment:

> [I]n the experience of the mirror, a moment can come about when the image we believe we abide by undergoes modification. If this specular image we have facing us, which is our stature, our face, our two eyes, allows the dimension of our gaze to emerge, the value of the image starts to change – above all if there's a moment when this gaze that appears in the mirror starts not to look at us anymore. There's an initium, an aura, a dawning sense of uncanniness which leaves the door open to anxiety. This passage from the specular image to the double that escapes me is the point at which something

occurs whose generality, whose presence within the entire phenomenal field, can be shown through the articulation we have been giving to the function of the *a*. This function goes far beyond what appears in this odd moment, which I simply wanted to mark out for its character of being at once the most commonly known and the most discreet in its intensity.[41]

Anxiety is both something that seems familiar (the most commonly known) and something that can escape us (discreet in its intensity). By using the French first-person plural pronoun (*nous*), Lacan presents this experience as something that can happen to anyone. We have now diverged significantly from the view of the human as a maladapted organism. Lacan's mirror introduces the dimension of otherness – the Other of language and the otherness of the semblable – as fundamental elements of human subjectivity. In this peculiar moment that opens the way to anxiety, our specular image becomes threateningly foreign, embodying an unfamiliar gaze. But what precisely is this gaze that appears in the specular image? Is it not merely *our* gaze? Lacan connects it to what he calls the 'function of the object *a*', introducing the idea that it represents the desiring gaze of the other. To grasp why the gaze in the specular image is not just our own gaze but assumes the quality of the desiring gaze of the other, and how the mirror image can be a source of anxiety, we need first to understand the significance that the mirror holds in Lacan's work.

Lacan considers the space of the mirror as pivotal in the formation of the ego. He directs our attention to the infant when it first succeeds in recognizing in the mirror image itself as a unified entity. Prior to this, the infant had not experienced its body as a totality that corresponds to (what we call) the 'I'; rather, the body had been experienced as a series of disconnected (although neither recognized as connected nor as disconnected) sources of excitation, painful or pleasant, often in a confused continuum with the body of the caretaker. Think for instance of breastfeeding, during which the boundaries between the mother's breast and the baby's body may be blurred.

During what Lacan calls the mirror stage, which unfolds over a series of moments, and marks an irreversible transformation, the fragmented sources of bodily sensations and body parts come together into a single unity called 'I'. Lacan remarks, however, that the formation of this 'I' always occurs within the context of a 'You'. The mother, or father, or whoever accompanies the child in front of that mirror looks at the child and the specular image and says, 'This is you!' Here several interconnected processes take place: the construction of the ego, its connection to the mirror image (referred to as the imaginary dimension), the introduction to the symbolic dimension of language, the emergence of desire, the perception of one's own body as the object of someone's gaze and desire. Lacan describes this stage as the moment when the body assumes its seductive and desired function.[42] The previous kind of enjoyment experienced by the body will undergo a lasting transformation, and the self will emerge as split or doubled at its core. The human body will no longer be a mere physical entity but will forever bear the marks of two dimensions: the symbolic dimension conveyed through the words 'this is you,' and the imaginary dimension characterized by a certain kind of misrecognition, where we see ourselves not only through the mirror's reflection but also through the gaze of others.

This gaze that beholds us as we behold ourselves, offering approval and recognition of our likeness, will persist throughout our lives, influencing our perception when we look at ourselves in the mirror. It shapes how we interpret our reflected image, whether we perceive ourselves as too tall or too short, too fat or too thin, prompting the question of 'too x in the eyes of whom?' Hence, what breaks down during moments of anxiety, as described by Lacan, is the familiar interplay of identification with others and the object of their gaze – what we may refer to as the play of desire. Lacan directly links anxiety to desire when he describes fantasy, which sustains desire, as an attempt to avoid anxiety, to keep 'a lid on it'.[43]

2.3.1 When there is no desiring gaze

In Lacan's work, the object of anxiety, known as 'object *a*', is not an actual object but a function. Its function is to generate desire by concealing castration (and revealing it through that concealment[44]). Certain objects can assume the function of object *a*, such as the breast, the voice, or the gaze. Because object *a* is not an actual object, when Lacan uses the paradoxical formulation that anxiety is not-without-an-object, he is not actually breaking away from the Kierkegaardian and Heideggerian tradition.

It may appear peculiar to the reader that the other's gaze, which observes my mirrored image and identifies it as 'you' (thus as me), is a desiring gaze. One might be inclined to view desire as a separate action, as if we first perceive the world and then desire it. However, Lacan's point is that we are inherently desiring beings, and we perceive the world through the lens of desire. The desiring gaze, which we may encounter when we observe our reflected image, supports the misrecognition that we lack nothing, that it is the other who is lacking something and seeks it within us: this is the function of object *a*.[45] Anxiety, for Lacan, arises when this initial misrecognition that occurs in identification with the mirror image breaks down. It occurs when the lack, which sustains the desiring gaze and thus our identity as desiring and desired beings, is lacking.[46]

Like 'not-without-an-object' the formulation 'the lack is lacking' may also seem paradoxical at first sight, as it challenges the intuitive connection between anxiety and the threat of loss (which Freud also draws). As discussed earlier,

Lacan's 'not-without-an-object' does not mean 'with an object' but 'with object *a*', which is a function, the function of simultaneously unconcealing and concealing what we lack. Now let us examine the idea that lack is lacking. Lacan agrees with Freud that anxiety serves as a signal. But whereas in Freud's reading, anxiety signals the danger of a loss (castration), Lacan says that anxiety is not a signal for the danger of castration but for the danger of the lack of castration. In other words, anxiety emerges not in the face of lack itself but in the face of the lack of lack.

Returning to the mirror, the absence of lack becomes apparent when the game of misrecognition collapses, leading to a sudden recognition of oneself outside the framework of misrecognition. Recall that when we observe ourselves in the mirror, the reflected image is always already mediated by the gaze of the other. The gaze of the other is ever-present; we see ourselves as we believe others see us, preparing ourselves for their gaze, while being observed by this internal other. Think of the cultural norms regarding attractiveness and how they shape our perception of our mirror image, or think of how the gaze of specific others, for whom we strive to appear attractive, accompanies us whenever we look at ourselves in the mirror ('How does my partner, parents, or friends see me?').

In other words, it is not the gaze of the other that shocks us or induces anxiety since that gaze is always present, familiar and part of the 'Heimlich'. The unfamiliar element must disrupt the ordinary process of looking at oneself through the gaze of the other and the misrecognition it typically entails. 'Lack is lacking' implies a temporary suspension of the typical interplay between desire and misrecognition. Lacan associates this with what he calls 'the Real', suggesting that in moments of anxiety before the mirror, we may encounter the materiality of our own body, an automaton-like aspect of ourselves, stripped of the desiring gaze of the other. It is this encounter with a stranger, with ourselves as a stranger (insofar as we are not perceived through the gaze of the other), that elicits a sense of anxiety.[47]

The characterization that 'lack is lacking' initially appears confusing because we typically associate lack with something negative and disruptive to the normal flow of things. On the surface, it seems more logical to suggest that anxiety arises when lack is present. However, it is important to remember that for Lacan, desire is driven by lack and is intimately related to it. Desire is structured around a constant movement from excitement to disappointment. Disappointment (lack, castration, prohibitions, etc.) is not external to desire but an inherent part of its function. In our everyday mode of being, we encounter lack continuously. This constant movement from excitement and hope to disappointment is our most familiar mode of being.

While we tend to associate anxiety with the lack of a specific object – such as the fear of illness, loss of a partner or job – these examples are closer to the phenomenon of fear. Contrary to the idea that anxiety arises when our ordinary life is disturbed and we encounter the unfamiliar, Lacan insightfully reminds us that anxiety arises when we gain insight into the fact that our ordinary everyday life is based on misrecognition. In Lacan's framework, this misrecognition primarily operates within the domain of desire, but it is essential to remember that, for him, desire is not a partial aspect of our lives; instead, desire structures our reality to such an extent that one could argue that reality itself is founded on misrecognition. This is why anxiety, unlike fear, can strike at any time and may not necessarily be connected to specific life-threatening or equilibrium-threatening experiences.

As a result, according to Lacan, anxiety is not a signal of lack but rather a signal of the failure of the support that lack provides.[48] This is the crucial point: lack offers a sense of familiarity and structure within the everyday. It cushions us from the realization that there is no specific way to structure our lives and identities. Lack and the support it provides are preferred because they are more familiar and structured compared to the unfamiliar realm of freedom.[49]

Lacan is right to think that anxiety cannot be explained solely in terms of an organism panicking when something crucial for its safety is lost. This is not to deny that we experience panic, anxiety, fear and worry when something dear to us is lost or when our physical and psychological well-being is threatened. However, understanding objectless anxiety requires a more nuanced understanding of the human experience. Lacan's starting point for understanding anxiety is not a life crisis but rather the simple act of looking at our mirror image. By reversing the conventional idea that anxiety arises when lack (the loss of an object) is imminent, Lacan proposes the seemingly counterintuitive notion that anxiety appears when lack is absent (when lack is lacking). From this perspective, anxiety becomes a manifestation of the fact that lack is 'man's home'.[50] It reveals that we are divided subjects, that the play of misrecognition – inherent in desire – structures our world, identity and relationships with others. We live our lives by imagining that there is always something we lack but will attain, or that we possess something special that others desire. In this pendulum movement from frustration to elation life goes by. For Lacan objectless anxiety occurs when we see our existence and ourselves outside of this oscillation, when we see the human existence in its finitude.

However, for Heidegger and Kierkegaard, anxiety does not merely signify an empty existence devoid of familiarity. Instead, they would add that when the usual play of desire is suspended, what emerges is also the possibility of existing apart from the game of misrecognition.

For both Heidegger and Kierkegaard this would gesture towards existential freedom, inviting us to recognize that we are cases of being-possible, characterized by openness. But for Lacan, such openness or freedom can only be seen as part of the play of desire that is suspended in anxiety – an illusion of sorts.

2.4 Anxiety as a glimpse at our openness

By using the concepts of *heimlich* (the familiar) and *unheimlich* (the unfamiliar), it is likely that Lacan engages in a conversation with Heidegger's ideas.[51] Undoubtedly, there is an overlap between Lacan's and Heidegger's descriptions of anxiety, as they both take anxiety to emerge when our ordinary way of being-in-the-world, what is most inconspicuously familiar, becomes unavailable or strange. In Lacan's example we look at ourselves in the mirror and what ordinarily sustains our perception of who we are, the desiring gaze of the other, is not there. In Heidegger's account, what usually engages us, the most simple and everyday ways in which entities and activities matter to us suddenly become unavailable. In both cases, we experience a sense of emptiness and estrangement from the world and ourselves, even though nothing has fundamentally changed, and there is no imminent loss of a beloved object. This is the essence of the *unheimlich*, the uncanny, the unfamiliar.

Indeed, in Heidegger's work, anxiety reveals the unfamiliar and strange nature of our existence, and we often find related descriptions in the Heideggerian literature, such as the idea that anxiety is occasioned by recognizing that the human existence (*Dasein*) is interpretation all the way down,[52] that it reveals the groundlessness of the world,[53] a universal meaninglessness,[54] a complete collapse of the structure of meaning in which one lives.[55,56] However, despite the overlap, there is an important difference between the two accounts that we can miss if we reduce Heidegger's anxiety to the above-mentioned descriptions. Whereas in Lacan's reading, the emergence of the unfamiliar is the final word in the anxiety story, in Heidegger's reading it is not.

Like Kierkegaard, Heidegger highlights as a defining trait of anxiety that it is caused by nothing in particular. When we are anxious, it is not in the face of any entity within the world, but something completely indefinite, 'what causes us anxiety is strictly speaking nowhere.'[57]

But Heidegger develops this idea in a direction that clearly distinguishes it from Lacan's perspective. He writes:

> [B]ut the obstinacy of the nowhere means as a phenomenon that the world as such is that in the face of which one has anxiety [...] what oppresses us is not this or that, nor is the summation of everything present-at-hand; it is rather [...] the world itself. [...] the most primordial 'something.'[58]

As remarked earlier, if no change has taken place on the level of entities, then the nothing that we encounter must be a result of the withdrawal of something that sustains our relation to entities but is not itself an entity. This is the simple fact that there is meaning at all, that things are present and intelligible. This 'most primordial' phenomenon about our human lives usually goes unnoticed, but in the case of anxiety, it comes to the forefront. In anxiety, it emerges in a negative manner, appearing as nothing and nowhere to be found, but this nowhere points (negatively) to the presence of meaning. To put it differently, the fact that anxiety is described as an encounter with nothing and the fact that anxiety is described as what reveals the givenness of meaning are not contradictory but complementary. That there is a world, that things appear to us in the first place, comes forth in anxiety, but it can only do so as a nothing from the perspective of entities, given that it is not a 'something' in the way entities are.

This significant difference from Lacan is also exemplified in Heidegger's characterization of the withdrawal that occurs in anxiety as simultaneously a 'turning towards us', a sign of presence.[59] What turns towards us is the inconspicuous but wondrous fact that we are in a world, that things appear to us, that we can make sense of them.[60] Anxiety is not solely an insight into groundlessness or the fact that reality (as structured by desire) is driven by misrecognition, as Lacan suggests. Instead, in Heidegger's description of anxiety, we find an affirmation of what sustains the human existence – the a priori presence of meaningfulness. The fact that we are beings that have access to 'the presencing of what is present'[61] and can transcend our everyday condition by 'shaping a world'[62] allows us to move a step further, beyond the state of existential homelessness (the *unheimlich*) towards *an urge to be at home everywhere.*[63]

This accounts for the more positive affective connotations that Heidegger and Kierkegaard attribute to anxiety and that I commented on in the beginning of this chapter. Because of what it reveals, anxiety is not only 'a reminder of what is dark and riddlesome in existence' but also of 'the brilliance surrounding whatever comes to light',[64] a reminder of what is possible for us. This is why the kind of anxiety herein discussed has within it an element of wonder.

3

Anxiety and the origin of human existence

3.1 Who are we and what are we for?

In the *Philosophical Fragments* Kierkegaard refers to a passage from Plato's *Phaedrus* where Socrates, otherwise 'a connoisseur of human nature',[1] appears utterly puzzled by it. In this passage Socrates appears reluctant – in response to a request by Phaedrus – to think about or explain various mythical theories and legends about the Gorgons, the Pegasuses, the Centaurs and the like, because, he says, he has no time for that and has a more urgent matter to attend to:

I myself have certainly no time for the business, and this is the reason why, my friend. I can't as yet 'know myself', in accordance with the Delphic inscription, and it seems ridiculous to me to inquire into other matters while I am still ignorant about that. Consequently, leaving such things aside, and accepting what is commonly believed about them, as I was saying just now, I aim my inquiry not to these but to myself, to see whether I am actually a beast more complex and more Typhonic than Typhon, or a tamer and simpler animal, sharing by nature some divine and un-Typhonic fate.[2]

Although Kierkegaard does not comment on the odd way in which Socrates phrases the question, it is worth paying attention to the strangeness of Socrates's question. Instead of an open question that corresponds to the inscription 'Know thyself' and asks 'Who am I?' Socrates offers a structured question with only two options, 'a beast more complex and more Typhonic than Typhon, or a tamer and simpler animal, sharing by nature some divine and un-Typhonic fate'.

This is not a psychological question about Socrates as an individual. As a philosopher Socrates knows that asking who he is is not possible without asking what a human being is, and vice versa. He knows in other words that self-knowledge and knowledge of the human nature go hand in hand. Nor are the Typhonic and the divine meant to be psychological characteristics, about how often he gets angry or how often he manages to retain his calm. If this were the case, it would be unclear why it should deserve all his attention and time. If we regarded these (the Typhonic and the divine) as psychological characteristics, then one could respond to him by saying, 'Well, sometimes you may be destructive and violent, other times you may be calm and tamer.' It could even seem unsophisticated and simplistic for him to be looking for *one* answer, as if he were a one-dimensional creature.[3]

Taking a distance from a psychological reading of the question, we should instead pause and remark on the fact that Socrates gives two unhuman options in response to a question about the nature of the human being. On the one hand, there is an image of a monster, Typhon, a destructive creature mentioned in Hesiod's *Theogony*. On the other hand, there is the divine fate, which is (puzzlingly) characterized as being a tamer and simpler animal. The strangeness of these options should alert us to the fact that this is not a case of narrowing down the options of what a human being is and then choosing one of two, for the very options Socrates offers are themselves perplexingly unhuman.[4] Socrates must aim his enquiry not at deciding for one of the two options, but at understanding what it means that the human existence is not fully at home in itself, in the first place. I understand this to mean that it has no definite direction and that, insofar as it doesn't, it can transcend itself through that questioning.

The kind of complexity that is at stake here, when asking the question about the nature of human existence, becomes clearer if we consider how one would go about answering it. For example, one could answer by referring to the defining traits of Homo Sapiens; or one could answer by referring to us as creatures of God in which case God's will (or plan for us) would define who we are; or one could answer by referring to us as rational animals and it would be the range of possibilities opened up by rationality that defines who we are, etc. But none of these (nor all of them together) can offer us a definite description of the human existence and this is because unlike other kinds of beings we are open-ended.

Thomas Sheehan describes this open-endedness by comparing and juxtaposing our existence to the being of a table-under-construction and the being of God.[5] On the one hand, we are like the table, insofar as we are an instance of becoming and there is a sense in which we are called to fulfil our possibilities. Yet we are also unlike the table, as the table's becoming ends when its construction reaches its goal. On the other hand, like God, we are already whole and perfect in the sense that there is no predetermined stage ahead that we are meant to reach, as we are not a step in a process of making – but, unlike God, we are whole and perfect in our incompleteness and finitude.

This essential open-endedness – reflected in the fact that none of the otherwise valid descriptions allows us to settle the question about the human – is related to our sense-making capacity. By making sense, we open possibilities, we become an activity of opening, but this very possibility of opening possibilities (the possibility of possibility, as Kierkegaard puts it) is also itself open-ended, in the sense that it precedes us and exceeds us (our individual existence), without any clue why or how it has arisen. As Heidegger puts it, this due to which humanity is as humanity in the first place eludes us: it is so near and yet so far.

> [T]he extent to which humanity is not at home in its own essence is betrayed by the opinion human beings cherish of themselves as those who have invented and who could have invented languages and understanding, building and poetry. How is humanity ever supposed to have invented that which pervades it in its sway, due to which humanity itself can be as humanity in the first place?[6].

The Concept of Anxiety asks a similar question to the one Heidegger asks in the above passage, when in a footnote to a discussion of the prohibition in the myth of the Fall, Kierkegaard (as Vigilius Haufniensis) discourages us from thinking of man as the inventor of language. Putting forward the idea that the voice of punishment comes from Adam himself (rather than God), Vigilius reminds us that the speaker (Adam in this case) *is* language and that if one asked the question how the first man learned to speak, we should reply that 'it will not do to represent man himself as the inventor of language'.[7]

In other words, that things make sense to us and appear as meaningful to us is not a matter of choice – language is not like the secret code one invents with their siblings so that the parents do not know what they are saying. That things have meaning (in the double sense of intelligibility and mattering) is a primordial fact that conditions all possibilities of understanding, let alone of codes. And it is not just a primordial fact that sits there in the background like some abstract condition. Heidegger uses the dynamic description 'pervades it in its sway' to describe its influence: everything we do – all our actions, achievements, daily life – is made possible by the fact that there is meaning at all.

3.2 Anxiety and spirit

If what pervades our essence cannot be reduced to anthropological, biological or theological facts about us, and if it has not been invented by us, then it must have a transcendent nature: hence it may appear as an unhuman element, like in the descriptions that Socrates offers, or as an enigmatic, mysterious element like in Heidegger's and Kierkegaard's aforementioned descriptions of the disclosive powers of language. Kierkegaard uses the concept of the 'moment' (Øieblikket in Danish, also translated as 'instant') to refer to the origin of the human existence as something that appears out of nowhere, that cannot be explained nor traced back to a sequence of events. In the *Philosophical Fragments*, Climacus distinguishes between a proper beginning and the kinds of beginnings we ordinarily encounter. The latter are not, strictly speaking, cases of beginning but they are cases of a transformation or change from one state to another state. The former is more like an Archimedean point, a beginning that cannot be derived from anything else, and Kierkegaard calls it 'coming-into-existence'. Although some beginnings are a case of movement from one state to another state ($\kappa \acute{\iota} \nu \eta \sigma \iota \varsigma$) or of change ($\alpha \lambda \lambda o \acute{\iota} \omega \sigma \iota \varsigma$) – think of the baby's coming into existence as a transformation from the state of being an embryo, and before that sperm and egg, and so on – there is also the beginning of 'what he calls coming into existence [which] would be absolutely different from any other change, because it would be no change at all, for every change has always presupposed a something'.[8] The moment is a case of this (radical) beginning where the emergence of possibility cannot be inferred from, or causally linked to, any previous state,[9] the gift or birth of presence.[10]

Interestingly, Kierkegaard uses this concept to describe both the strange origin of the human existence, that humanity is the gift of presence that emerged suddenly and mysteriously, and the particular instances of objectless anxiety and wonder that reconnect us with the mysteriousness of our origin. It is because our origin has the characteristics of what he calls the 'moment' that Socrates can only come up with what looks like unhuman options for who we are. And it is because certain moods, like anxiety and wonder, give us access to this strange origin that they also take the form of the 'moment'.[11] The qualification 'moment' captures their swift, sudden and vanishing character – such experiences appear out of nowhere, seize us momentarily and then vanish into nothing again – but it also captures the fact that they bear witness to a transcendent[12] element of the human existence.[13]

Kierkegaard often uses the term 'spirit' for this transcendent dimension of our existence which can manifest itself in the fashion of a 'moment'[14]: 'as soon as the spirit is posited, the moment is present'.[15] 'Spirit' is not an easy concept to explain, but for our purposes here we can say that it holds the tension between body and soul, the physical and the psychical, the temporal and the eternal, the finite and the infinite in us. It sustains their synthesis but in a way that keeps alive the contradictions, hence Haufniensis also calls spirit 'a hostile power, for it constantly disturbs the relation between body and soul'.[16] This is why we should not think of 'spirit' in static terms, as a separate layer of our being, but in dynamic terms: spirit is a category of relationality, it is the way in which the contradictions in our being – finite and infinite, man and animal, etc. – relate to each other and we relate to them. These contradictions of our condition and the resulting disunity are the condition for our access to possibility: it is because we are open-ended – neither only finite nor only infinite, neither only body nor only soul – that we can be open.

It is within this context that Kierkegaard's account of anxiety is situated: anxiety is the way we relate to the 'ambiguous power' of spirit,[17] an affective manifestation of the aforementioned tension. Anxiety embodies the simultaneous attraction and repulsion that the human existence 'feels' towards its transcendent element, the tension between our finite and infinite dimensions. As a result, anxiety cannot be understood solely through an empirical science because it is a manifestation of the spiritual component of the human existence. When Kierkegaard attempts to offer a psychological account of the kind of anxiety he has in mind, he must also reshape psychology so that it has space for spirit, given that as an empirical science, psychology can only have access to body and psyche. Kierkegaard is looking for 'an adequate psychology of anxiety', and psychology as such can only be inadequate, he thinks, to the extent that it overlooks the dimension of spirit in the human being and only sees the human as an antithesis between body and psyche.[18]

3.3 Adam as our origin

Recall that in the question about who he is, Socrates comes up with two un-human options, a monster like Typhon or a case of the divine. I took this to reflect that something about our condition is, as I called it, transcendent: it is neither derivable from nor reducible to any fact within our existence, and yet it conditions our existence. Similarly, Kierkegaard turns to a myth to tell a story about our origin as a 'moment', namely as a beginning that is enigmatic and does not derive from any particular fact. This is the myth of Genesis. In order to understand why one should even begin to take a myth[19] seriously as a valid source of knowledge about the human condition, we must distinguish the myth both from the real and the fantastic. A myth is neither an empirically testable story about our history nor a pure product of fiction. A myth is the expression of an insight about who we are: 'the myth allows something that is inward to take place outwardly'.[20]

Kierkegaard picks the myth of the Fall, in which sin has a central place.[21] As mentioned before, this is important because it shows that our origin (our structural features) is intertwined with a task that we are called to fulfil. Anxiety and sinfulness are therefore deeply connected in his account: anxiety is 'the presupposition of hereditary sin' and explains 'hereditary sin progressively in terms of its origin'.[22] In Kierkegaard's reading, anxiety *is* the original sin, in the sense that it expresses Adam's (as well as our own) ambivalence towards the capacity for spirit, an ambivalence that can take the form of a fleeing-from, or a forgetfulness (in our everyday life).

Given that the myth is what allows what is inward to take place outwards, Adam is not outside our history and his sin is not something external to us; instead, Adam is an expression of the state of every individual – my state, the reader's state, Socrates's state, Kierkegaard's state, etc. This is because of 'what is essential to human existence: that man is *individuum* and as such simultaneously himself and the whole race, and in such a way that the whole race participates in the individual and the individual participates in the race'.[23] The term 'human race' is how Kierkegaard refers to what today we would call 'humanity' or 'humanness'. If the original sin is an Archimedean point that cannot be derived from anything else, then Adam is an archetype rather than a deterministic explanation of the human condition.[24] Adam is at the same time 'himself and the race', and 'Adam's sin must be essentially human sin so that whatever explains the sin of one explains the sin of all'.[25]

Anxiety links every individual to Adam, to this mythical figure whose story embodies our constitutional features. It does so because it has a double role: it lies in our origin (it is an ontological feature),[26] but it also appears within the individual life (it is an ontic state that offers an ontological insight). As an affective phenomenon that can occur in the life of any individual, it connects every individual 'back'[27] to Adam as an archetype of the human condition. To explain how it is possible for every individual to share the same psychological phenomenon with Adam who has sinned, Kierkegaard must also challenge the traditional reading of prohibition, sin, and punishment, according to which God prohibited eating the fruit of the Tree of Knowledge, Adam chose not to listen, and, as a result of that decision, he was expelled from Paradise. For

Vigilius Haufniensis, neither the prohibition nor the temptation could have come from God. Adam would not understand the prohibition, because surely knowledge of good and evil would follow as a consequence of eating the fruit. Further, Adam would not understand the word of judgement – 'You shall certainly die' – as he does not yet know what it means to die. Finally, God could not have tempted Adam, as God 'tempts no man and is not tempted by anyone, but each person is tempted by himself'[28]:

> When it is stated in Genesis that God said to Adam 'only from the tree of the knowledge of good and evil you must not eat' it follows as a matter of course that Adam really has not understood this word, for how could he understand the difference between good and evil when this distinction would follow as a consequence of the enjoyment of the fruit? When it is assumed that the prohibition awakens the desire, one acquires knowledge instead of ignorance, and in that case Adam must have had a knowledge of freedom, because the desire was to use it. The explanation is therefore subsequent. The prohibition induces in him anxiety, for the prohibition awakens in him freedom's possibility. What passed by innocence as the nothing of anxiety has now entered into Adam, and here again it is a nothing – the anxious possibility of being able.[29]

What Kierkegaard's reading dispels – in multiple ways that this chapter cannot begin to do justice to – is a simplistic distinction between a state before-the-sin and a state after-the-sin. For Kierkegaard, anxiety permeates even the state of innocence (qua ignorance), because innocence is like a state of suspension, a waiting for something: 'this is the profound secret of innocence that it is at the same time anxiety'.[30] The prohibition that Adam cannot fully understand awakens something that was already there, namely, anxiety: 'Because Adam has not understood what was spoken, there is nothing but the ambiguity of anxiety'.[31] Although Adam cannot understand the prohibition fully, the prohibition awakens 'the infinite possibility of being able'[32] and this awakens anxiety. The 'you must not' carries within it a 'you can' and it becomes a reminder that Adam (the human existence) is essentially open. Neither spirit nor anxiety is introduced with the prohibition; rather, they are both there even in the state of innocence, but not yet awake. Kierkegaard uses the beautiful term 'dreaming' to qualify the inactive state that awaits: 'In innocence anxiety is a qualification of dreaming spirit and as such it has its place in psychology.'[33] Innocent anxiety is a determination of dreaming spirit: in innocence, Adam as spirit was a dreaming spirit.[34]

The prohibition awakens the dreaming spirit and by doing so, it awakens anxiety too. But it is not Adam's decision that constitutes the sin; rather, the very presence of anxiety as an attraction towards and repulsion from spirit is the manifestation of sin, as it is a sign that Adam is away from spirit. Adam's ambivalence and our own ambivalence towards spirit manifest themselves in anxiety as a structural feature of existence. Spirit and possibility attract us and repel us at the same time; hence, humanity is in its essence in ambiguity, out of joint and anxious, but also in wonder and open towards possibility.

Anxiety lies in the origin of sin and the beginning of the human condition, but it also further reinforces that condition. Sin and anxiety have a loop-like structure: 'Sin entered in anxiety, but sin in turn brought anxiety along with it'.[35] If in Adam's case there was sin, in our case there is sinfulness – a sinfulness that starts with Adam's anxiety but reproduces itself as sin brings more anxiety. 'The concept of anxiety is supposed to explain the irruption of sin[36] both retrogressively in terms of its origin, and progressively in terms of its continual rebirth'.[37] This brings us to the phenomenon of anxiety in our individual lives.

3.4 Anxiety in the individual life, an insight into our origin

As suggested earlier, self-knowledge and knowledge about the human existence must be interconnected: one cannot set out to know what it means to be human without setting out to know oneself, and one cannot know oneself without addressing the question of what it means to be human. Hence Socrates asks the question in the first person and aims his enquiry at himself. That this question can only be approached from the first person can explain why answering it does not involve the accumulation of knowledge or historical progress, unlike scientific questions that can be asked in a third-personal manner and can be answered progressively by different researchers.

Anxiety is the mood, the psychological phenomenon, that connects every individual with Adam, a mythical figure that acts as an archetype for who we are. As mentioned earlier, anxiety, for Kierkegaard, plays a double role: it is an ontic phenomenon, the mood of anxiety that strikes once in a while in the life of an individual, and it is also an ontological feature of our existence.[38] The former points to the latter. Qua experience within the individual life, anxiety works as 'a fundamental mode of affective self-awareness,'[39] offering us an insight into our constitutional access to and ambivalence towards spirit. In other words, the experience of anxiety here and now in one's individual life reflects a structural anxiety in the face of possibility.

As in Adam's case, anxiety is, for the individual, a response to the simultaneous attraction and repulsion that spirit or possibility creates, a sign that we are near it and far from it at the same time.[40] Once again, spirit or possibility is in a certain sense 'nothing'. They do not have the character of a something, of an entity in the world or of what Kierkegaard would call cases of actuality: 'A person is thus anxious about "nothing," "nothing" as understood as the non-actual.'[41] This simultaneous attraction and repulsion, as well as the fact that what we encounter oscillates between a presence that overwhelms us and an absence, a nothing, that we cannot grasp, find expression in the metaphor of dizziness.

> Anxiety may be compared with dizziness. He whose eye happens to look down into the yawning abyss becomes dizzy. But what is the reason for this? It is just as much in his own eye as in the abyss, for suppose he had not looked down. Hence anxiety is the dizziness of freedom, which emerges when the spirit wants to posit the synthesis and freedom looks down into its own possibility, laying hold of finiteness to support itself. Freedom succumbs in this dizziness. Further than this, psychology cannot and will not go.[42]

The infinite power of being able – spirit – attracts us and repels us at the same time: hence, we cannot but look down. The phenomenon of vertigo is illuminating. Think of the case when, while standing at the edge of a cliff, we may feel terrified of falling,[43] yet part of the fear is that we may fall without being pushed, as if what lies over the cliff could have some strange kind of attraction or pull over us. This is the phenomenon that Kierkegaard finds most illuminating when he tries to explain anxiety. In anxiety we are attracted by the very thing we are terrified of. This, in Kierkegaard's terms, is the freedom that our access to possibility involves. This experience of vertigo shows both our attraction to freedom and our distance from freedom, the fact that we fear it. Anxiety is entangled freedom,[44] as Vigilius Haufniensis characteristically puts it. This is how anxiety as an experience can connect us to our origin; by experiencing anxiety in one's individual life, one comes to know that the human existence is structurally anxious because it is structurally a case of entangled freedom. We learn that we are cases of openness but that we are also forgetful of it, distanced from it. In anxiety and wonder, this capacity for openness and possibility – part of our constitution but also simultaneously a task – lights up for us.

4

Wonder and the origin of philosophy

4.1 Wonder at the most usual unusual

Like in the case of 'anxiety', a wonder that finds wondrous not 'this' or 'that' but the entirety of the world, can seem strange as it challenges our customary understanding of emotions. Indeed, in ordinary life we often use the word 'wonder' in response to unusual things around us. Examples vary, from a beautiful body, or someone's drawing skills, to the universe and how it came to be. Such cases are linked to what is challenging to know and explain or to features that we admire and would like to possess, like a skill or a talent.[1] Relatedly, ordinary wonder can be a response not only to an epistemic deficit (what we do not understand) but also to an epistemic achievement (what we come to know or discover).

We wonder, for example, at a rainbow as a baffling phenomenon, but we also wonder at its explanation when we learn what brings it about. Despite the variations in the range of cases described, there is a feature they all share: they are responses to unusual entities or unusual traits of entities. Although the degree of the unusualness and how we relate to it – whether we can and want to be like it, or whether we can and want to explain it away – may vary, there is always an entity (a person, a skill, a natural phenomenon) that stands out through its unusualness.

However, unlike the above cases of wonder, there are moments when wonder strikes us without a specific object of focus, when 'anything whatsoever as such and everything as everything'[2] fills us with awe. Here, the notion of 'everything' does not imply a mere accumulation of individual entities, nor does it suggest that every single thing becomes imbued with wonder. Rather, objectless wonder emerges when the totality that underpins our engagement with the world emerges into view.[3] When we wonder in this way, although nothing has changed, entities as such and as a whole appear in a different light: we see everything against the background fact that there is meaning at all, that we make sense of them and they make sense to us.

If someone asks us what it is exactly that we wonder at, we may, like Wittgenstein in an example I discuss later in the book, come up with phrases such as 'at the fact that anything exists in the first place'. However, because there is hardly any novelty involved in this idea, our object of wonder also, at the same time, seems to peter out into nothing. Because there seems to be no specific unusual (trait of an) entity that causes the wonder, such moments can feel both significant and trivial at the same time. To avoid the threat of triviality, one may even try to turn this odd wonder into the ordinary versions I mentioned earlier; one may think, for example, that wonder at the fact that the world is and that we are at all corresponds to wonder at the Big Bang, at how matter came into existence. But as a scientific question, this is not only something unusual but also something that admits an answer, a case where epistemic deficit and achievement is involved.

Such attempts would not stay true to the experience: the kind of wonder I focus on here is in response to something that looks very unusual and very usual at the same time – strange yet familiar. What fills us with wonder in such cases is not that things have come to exist but that they are intelligible in the first place. Heidegger aptly describes the object of this wonder as 'the most usual unusual'. Unlike the more typical instances of wonder, there is no specific entity that evokes our wonder, and there is nothing extraordinary about any particular entity. Here the object of wonder is instead the most usual but which now looks as the most unusual: 'In wonder, what is most usual of all and in all, i.e. *everything*, becomes the most unusual [...] in this one respect: that it is what it is.'[4]

Due to the peculiar nature of this wonder, we find ourselves in a particularly passive state. Unlike other instances of wonder that we actively attempt to resolve, this kind of wonder leaves us in a state of passivity. Heidegger captures this aspect when he suggests that there is no entry point into the unusualness of what is most usual, nor is there an exit from it.[5] Unlike the other forms of wonder that we can actively pursue and encounter at the circus, during a quantum physics lesson, in a book about the Seven Wonders of the World, or during a motorcycle race, this particular kind of wonder lacks an identifiable entry point. There is no worldly entity or fact to direct our attention towards in order to experience wonder. Likewise, unlike other types of wonder where we can emerge from the state of wonderment by acquiring knowledge about the perplexing subject or by attaining the admired skill, here the way out is not clear.

While this form of wonder may seem pointless, as it does not appear to lead to any specific knowledge acquisition or mastery of skills, Plato famously situates it at the origin of philosophy. Why? What does it mean that we are philosophical beings to the extent that we can experience wonder in this peculiar manner?

4.2 From rainbows to meaningfulness: Where philosophy begins

That wonder is the origin of philosophy is a familiar and old idea. It comes up both in Plato and in Aristotle: 'For this passion, wondering [θαυμάζειν], is the true mark of a philosopher. There is no other origin of philosophy than this one',[6] Plato's Socrates remarks in the *Theaetetus*; 'it is because of wondering [θαυμάζειν] at things that humans, both now and at first, began to do philosophy', we read in Aristotle's *Metaphysics*[7].

The tension between the two forms of wonder that I introduced earlier – wonder at something unusual versus wonder at the most usual unusual – is beautifully captured in a phrase that Plato adds to Socrates's remark on wonder as the origin of philosophy. Socrates continues, 'And I think he who said that Iris [Rainbow, or messenger] is the daughter of Thaumas [Wonderer] was not a bad genealogist.' Hannah Arendt notes that Iris signifies rainbow, but derived from the Greek εἴρειν (to tell), it can also refer to the phenomenon of speech and meaningful words (ρήματα).[8] These two interpretations suggest two distinct types of wonder: the rainbow aligns with wonder at something rare and unusual that prompts us to learn about it (what a rainbow is, when it appears, etc.), while the phenomena of speech, meaningfulness and sense are closer to the most usual unusual. Meaningfulness is the most usual because we always find ourselves within it, and the most unusual because its essence and origins remain a mystery. As Sheehan points out, we can make sense of everything except why we can make sense of anything in the first place.[9] These two aspects of wonder correspond to the difference between the nature and function of wonder in science and the nature and function of wonder in philosophy. Wonder as aporia – 'being puzzled on account of ignorance, which can be dispelled by knowledge'[10] – is closer to the rainbow interpretation of the passage and thus more aligned with the nature of wonder in the realm of science. Here, however, I will focus on the second interpretation. I am interested in the peculiar wonder at the fact that there is meaning in the first place, and I will explore how this connects to the origin of philosophy, why Socrates suggests that this is where philosophy originates.

In the Platonic dialogue *Theaetetus*, Socrates meets a young boy, Theaetetus, who has the reputation of being an exceptional student at the gymnasium. Wanting to witness and test his exceptional character and promising thinking skills, Socrates invites him to think about the relation between knowledge and wisdom, and what knowledge really is.

In his initial reply, Theaetetus offers examples of knowledge (such as geometry and shoemaking). Socrates is not pleased: '[Y]ou were not asked which things knowledge is of, nor how many kinds of knowledge there are, [but] what, exactly, knowledge is.'[11] He shows Theaetetus what he means through the example of clay: it is as if when asked what clay is, Theaetetus had replied 'potter's clay, oven-maker's clay, brick-maker's clay', instead of the 'simple thing': earth mixed with water. This is important: the fact that what is at stake in defining knowledge are different kinds of knowledge (not just propositional knowledge but also geometry and shoemaking) calls for caution around how to read Socrates's insistence on giving a final, universal definition of knowledge. Heidegger's own suggestion is that Socrates is not enquiring into necessary and sufficient conditions for knowing, but rather into something more fundamental: what it means to know *truly*, what brings things into unconcealment (ἀ-λήθεια) in the first place (hence the dialogue begins with the connection between wisdom and knowledge).

Theaetetus, courageous and honest, tries again. He offers a definition of knowledge as perception, which we could summarize in the following way: to know is to perceive, to have access to what directly appears to us.[12] Socrates then proposes to examine this view and its consequences in detail, using examples to show that 'that something *is*' cannot be derived from appearances. After getting Theaetetus to agree that nothing can become larger or smaller as long as it is equal to itself,[13] he presents him with a case where Socrates, while being just this size, without growing or shrinking, can within the space of a year be both larger than Theaetetus and smaller than him – not because Socrates has lost any of his size but because Theaetetus has grown. It is in response to this remark that the Platonic remarks on wonder come up:

> Th.: And by the gods, Socrates, I really wonder (θαυμάζω) at what these are and sometimes when I look at the truth of them I feel vertiginous. (**σκοτοδινιῶ**)

> S: Theodorus has not made at all a bad guess about your
> nature. For this passion,[14] wondering, is the true mark of
> a philosopher. There is no other origin of philosophy than
> this one. And I think he who said that Iris [Rainbow, or
> messenger] is the daughter of Thaumas [Wonderer] was
> not a bad genealogist.

It is noteworthy that for Plato, the wonder that serves as the origin of philosophy contains an essential element of dizziness. Theaetetus experiences not only wonder but also a sense of vertigo in the face of what he encounters.[15] The wonder from which philosophy originates is characterized by a vertiginous quality. While we will revisit the element of vertigo later, it is important to also note that Plato does not specify what precisely Theaetetus wonders at.[16]

4.3 Heidegger's reading of the *Theaetetus*: The wonder at 'that it is'

We may be tempted to think that Theaetetus feels wonder at the fact that what he thought he knew was not the case, at his epistemic deficit, or at the fact that he *thought* he knew.[17] But the text suggests that it is something about the truth (ἀληθῶς βλέπων) of what Socrates has presented that has a grip on the young Theaetetus. We may also be tempted to think that

Theaetetus wonders at how appearances can trick us. But the idea that one may look taller when compared to one's short friend, without having become taller, would hardly evoke the sense of wonder and dizziness that Theaetetus describes.

In his interpretation of *Theaetetus*,[18] Heidegger draws attention to the central role that *being* plays in the above remarks, and he directs our attention to the fact that soon after that remark on wonder, Socrates and Theaetetus discuss sound and colour as paradigmatic cases of appearing (φαίνεσθαι). Whereas sound and colour have designated organs in the body – ears and eyes – to perceive them, there is something that we perceive when we perceive sound and colour that precedes their specific appearances: this is the recognition 'that they both are'. Here is the relevant passage[19]:

> S: In regard to sound and colour: don't you first of all
>   perceive, taking them in, that they both are?
> Th: Yes.
> S: [...] the faculty that somehow provides a passage-way,
>   reveals to you what is common to your perceptions of
>   colour, sound, and everything else, and which you call 'is'
>   and 'is not'. With what sense organs do you perceive this
>   common element?
> [...]

> Th: [...] it seems to me that there is no special organ for this as there are for others, but the soul itself views, through itself, what all things have in common.

What all things have in common is that they *are*; what is common, Socrates says, is the 'is' and 'is not' – and from this follow features such as identity and non-identity, sameness and difference. When I perceive the green leaves of a tree, I am already perceiving something prior to the particular colour, namely, *that it is*, and I cannot perceive *how something is* unless I also perceive *that it is*. 'That it is' is prior. This 'that it is' allows me to have access to any entity under consideration (for instance, the green leaves of the tree), and thus enables me to assert the truth of my logos (what I say) regarding it.[20] Arendt agrees that it is the inconspicuous but omnipresent character of being that causes Theaetetus's wonder:

> The wonder that befalls the philosopher can never concern anything particular but is always aroused by the whole, which, in contrast to the sum total of entities, is never manifest. [...] Since Parmenides, the key word for this invisible imperceptible whole implicitly manifest in all that appears has been Being – seemingly the most empty and general, the least meaningful word in our vocabulary.[21]

What matters here is not just the verb 'to be', after all there are cultures that do not have a word for that.[22] What matters is that before we make any claims about the world, and perceive any particular things in particular situations, we are already facing a meaningful world, things are already present to us. This fundamental but very subtle presence that is prior to any particular dealings with things can be summarized in an equally central and inconspicuous grammatical form: things *are*. Later in the dialogue, Socrates imagines a scenario in which we get rid of being and substitute it with becoming. Doing so, he thinks, would also mean getting rid of words like 'something', 'someone's', 'my', 'this', 'that', namely words that 'bring things to a standstill' (ἵστασθαι). The 'that it is' that is prior to the 'how it is' is the simple fact that things can stand still and be present for us to perceive them in their specific 'how'. Once again, 'that things are' does not mean 'that they exist' (we can make claims about non-existent things); 'that they are' means that they can be made sense of, that they are intelligible. To put it in Greek terms, that they are **ὄντα** (beings) is another way to say that they are παρόντα (present),[23] available for ἀλήθεια (unconcealment, truth). By 'being', then, we should hear 'the meaningful':

The meaningful – that is what is first and immediately given to you without any mental detour through a conceptual grasp of the thing. When you live in the first-hand world, everything comes at you loaded with meaning, all over the place and all the time. Everything appears within a meaningful context, and that context gives those things their meaning.[24]

This focus on intelligibility, on 'the meaning of the meaningful'[25] explains why, according to Heidegger's reading of the *Theaetetus*, this kind of wonder appears in a dialogue that focuses on 'the essence of truth'.[26]

Yet what allows for things to stand still does not stand still itself, as it seems to elude our grasp the moment we attempt to apprehend it. The fact 'that things are' (that there is meaning) is so inextricably bound to the particular entities that when we try to separate the givenness of meaning from the entity or entities that we apprehend, it seems to evaporate in thin air, 'as if we were reaching into a void': what we discover is 'nothing actual, tangible, real'.[27] It is in this profound encounter with something intangible and unreal that we find an explanation for why this wonder is not merely a source of joy or pleasure. As previously mentioned, Plato describes this wonder as vertiginous. Just as vertigo creates the sensation of a spinning world without any visible motion, here we are profoundly moved by 'nothing actual'. This experience of dizziness serves as a bridge that connects wonder to anxiety; recall that Kierkegaard describes anxiety as dizziness. It also connects wonder to the manner in which philosophical thinking operates. Philosophical questions take a circular form, where one question begets another, and yet another, without the possibility of linear progress. This is because philosophy lacks an ultimate explanation or a singular starting point from which we can explain what mostly puzzles it, the claims that logos (speaking and meaning) make on us. 'This circling movement of philosophy', as Heidegger comments, 'makes us feel dizzy, and dizziness is something uncanny. We feel as though we are suspended in the Nothing'.[28] If philosophy's object is in some sense the nothing – insofar as its object is intelligibility – then wonder is its origin not because doing philosophy arises from curiosity, but because of the intrinsic 'inexplicability of philosophy, inexplicability in the sense that here in general to explain and the will to explain are mistakes'.[29]

4.4 Anxious wonder

The element of dizziness that is shared by the experiences of wonder and of anxiety is one way to think about the proximity of the two attunements. This proximity comes up both in Heidegger's and in Kierkegaard's works. Heidegger mentions wonder in his descriptions of anxiety[30] and Kierkegaard[31] links the two through the concept of 'moment', regarding both as cases of a sudden interruption of our actual lives by the possibility of possibility.

This proximity between anxiety and wonder may seem peculiar given our modern tendency to look at emotional life in the binary terms of positive or negative, uplifting or depressing. One might question how something distressing like anxiety can contain an uplifting element, or how a positive experience like wonder can possess a negative aspect. But language can help guide us out of this difficulty, pointing to a more complex view of the affective life: what is full of awe can be awful; what is terrific is also what evokes terror; and the word 'wonder' links etymologically to being wounded.[32]

This affective complexity reflects, in this case, the complexity of what is at stake in wonder and anxiety, namely the complex status of the presence of meaningfulness. In anxiety we encounter this presence as withdrawn, revealing itself to us in a negative manner, as a concealed aspect. Hence, anxiety can encompass not only distress but also joy or awe when we realize that we simultaneously face a previously hidden possibility – our openness to meaning. In the state of wonder, we catch a glimpse of meaningfulness not as something withdrawn but as an overflowing abundance. However, this awe-inspiring excess also brings forth two intertwined sensations. First, it evokes an uncanny feeling of being unable to point to the object of our wonder – it is simultaneously everywhere and nowhere – which contributes to the vertiginous nature of wonder. Second, it carries an anxious awareness that we possess a capacity that may be overlooked or forgotten. Third, it carries an anxious awareness that this capacity is finite, that it will end for each individual when they die. In other words, in wonder, we may experience both awe at our sense-making capacity and concern for its fragility.[33,34]

The shared ontological insight offered by wonder and anxiety puts us in a similar position in both cases: we become questioners.[35] Through this questioning we are opened to philosophy.[36] This convergence further underscores their affinity, as they both have the potential to give rise to the activity of philosophy. Earlier, we looked at Plato's idea that philosophy originates in dizzy wonder. Likewise, Kierkegaard writes that whoever educates themselves in anxiety becomes someone who cultivates philosophy on their own.[37] Heidegger also acknowledges that the fundamental question of philosophy emerges from both wonder and anxiety.[38]

Although we often refer to philosophy in a narrow sense, as an academic and professional activity – a systematic theoretical investigation, a primarily intellectual activity of analysing concepts, drawing distinctions and offering theories about how concepts work or what grounds them – we can also think of philosophy in broader terms, if we ask ourselves what it means that we can do philosophy in the first place. We find this broader sense in Plato's *Phaedrus*, for example, where we read that by nature the human mind dwells in philosophy,[39] and in Heidegger when he says that metaphysics belongs to the nature of the human being. 'It is neither a division of academic philosophy nor a field of arbitrary notions.'[40]

But what does it mean to regard philosophy as a natural dwelling place for the human being, when not everyone goes about to pursue philosophical questions? What I propose here is that philosophy is a capacity to experience the ontological insight that we get from encounters like wonder and anxiety. As such it is a prerequisite for the more systematic pursuing of questions around presencing and truth, to the extent that to pursue philosophical questions (in a narrower sense) is to explore the world according to its *logos*, namely to explore the world as present and, further, to explore how presencing works (for example, how the space of reasons works, what counts as truthfulness in different domains of life, or what specific structure truth takes in each case). Entering philosophy requires a realization that what is real (ὄν) and what is present to us (παρόν) coincide. The world is given to us as intelligible and this is where philosophy begins, in the givenness-gift of meaning. In the states of wonder and anxiety, this most ordinary and familiar aspect of our existence – that there is meaning – becomes the most extraordinary, and prompts us to question our own being, to see our existence in the light of the fact that there is meaning and we are world-forming. This particular characteristic of their insight explains their role in the origin of philosophy and underscores their close affinity.[41]

For Heidegger, that philosophy can originate in wonder and anxiety means that philosophical questioning can arise when we are exposed to these strange objectless moods. He summarizes this original philosophical questioning through what he calls the fundamental question of metaphysics, 'Why are there beings at all rather than nothing?' It is a difficult question to understand, and I can only make a brief reference to it here. Heidegger has deliberately chosen to rephrase a question that is famous in the history of philosophy: 'why is there something, rather than nothing?' Perhaps this is because he thought that working through certain familiar echoes of the question can help avoid some usual misunderstandings of the primary aim of philosophy. For example, if the question is not mistaken for a purely scientific enquiry such as 'What caused the emergence of matter?', it might be misinterpreted as an expression of extreme sceptical doubt. The question then would take the form 'How did existence arise from nothing, and how can we ensure that it will not vanish into nothingness once again?'.

In some respects, it may seem tempting to view the origin of philosophy as a quest for a secure foundation – for knowledge, existence or meaning. Consider, for instance, Leibniz's treatment of 'Why are there beings rather than nothing?' as equivalent to 'What caused beings to be?' – an enquiry seeking a secure cause that, for Leibniz, lies in God. Similarly, Descartes's postulation of substance can be understood as a means to escape profound doubt about the external world's existence and safeguard beings against the spectre of nothing that haunts the realm of sensory experience. In this case, the question can be interpreted as follows: How can we ensure the existence of beings against the threat of nothingness?[42] Such readings fit the idea of philosophy as a theory that aims to ground our knowledge, experience, meaning, namely as a fight against scepticism.

But Heidegger distances himself from the above reading of what distinguishes the philosophical activity. Instead, he emphasizes the primacy of questioning without seeking explanations, which may be a preamble to his later emphasis on the link between philosophy and poetry. He remarks that the fundamental question of philosophy is not motivated by a desire for explanation or the elimination of the extraordinary fact that beings are what they are. Rather, it represents an even more pure adherence to beings in their extraordinariness.[43] Heidegger's formulation of 'Why are there beings rather than nothing?' does not invite a search for a foundation against groundlessness. Instead of agonizing over the threat of non-existence or groundlessness, it directs us to marvel at the givenness of meaning. Hence the 'why' in the question is not a search for an explanation but an acknowledgement of the mystery of meaningfulness, 'an act of celebration', as Richard Polt puts it.[44] There was no necessity for meaning to arise or for the human to be thrown in meaning, and yet we are essentially sense-makers. This is not about 'seeking an origin or source that is temporally prior or physically more basic'[45] but about seeing the human life against the fact that we are sense-makers.[46] It is there that philosophy, as the natural dwelling place of the human, begins.

5

The paradox of anxiety and wonder

5.1 Seeing the world as a miracle, and the problem of nonsense

In the course of this book, in an attempt to describe what takes place in such moods of anxious wonder, terms that may sound paradoxical have been a regular occurrence. For example, anxiety and wonder have not only been described as objectless experiences, but also as experiences that take nothing[1] as their object. Lacan comes up with the strange phrases 'not without an object' and 'the lack is lacking' to describe the objectlessness of anxiety. And Heidegger describes extreme wonder as wonder at the most usual unusual. These are only some examples of the linguistic and expressive challenges these moods have presented us with.

Heidegger and Kierkegaard are not only conscious of the paradoxes these encounters entail, but they also seem to deem this paradoxicality fitting. Kierkegaard characterizes 'the moment' as a paradox. Heidegger comments on the apparent violation of logical rules when investigating anxiety as an encounter with nothing. However, in philosophy, especially since the so-called linguistic turn, paradoxicality is often equated with an absence of logical clarity and a subsequent worry about the validity of the expressions involved.[2] In Kierkegaard's case, scholars have questioned whether his 'paradox' entails a clash with reason,[3] while Heidegger's discussion around anxiety and the nothing has been dismissed as nonsensical pseudo-statements.[4]

Ludwig Wittgenstein problematizes the paradoxicality of wonder and anxiety in a 1929 remark that brings together Kierkegaard's paradox and Heidegger's concept of anxiety with his own example of wonder at the fact that anything exists.[5] He portrays the paradoxes of wonder and anxiety as instances of running up against the limits of language.[6] When Wittgenstein brings together Heidegger's anxiety and Kierkegaard's paradox as instances of what he calls a priori nonsense, he refers to the example of the astonishment that anything exists. This is an example he had previously discussed in a lecture he delivered the same year, known as 'A Lecture on Ethics'. There he also spoke of other similar experiences, like the sudden sense of feeling absolutely safe, as if nothing could harm us. The similarity of his description of wonder to the ones I discussed previously is striking:

I believe the best way of describing it is to say that when I have it, I wonder at the existence of the world. And I am then inclined to use such phrases as 'how extraordinary that anything should exist' or 'how extraordinary that the world should exist'. If I say 'I wonder at the existence of the world' *I am misusing language*. Let me explain this: It makes perfectly good and clear sense to say that I wonder at something being the case, we all understand what it means to say that I wonder at the size of a dog which is bigger than any one I have ever seen before or at any thing which, in the common sense of the word, is extraordinary. In every such case I wonder at something being the case which I could conceive not to be the case. [...] To say 'I wonder at such and such being the case' has only sense if I can imagine it not to be the case. In this sense one can wonder at the existence of, say, a house when one sees it and has not visited it for a long time and has imagined that it had been pulled down in the meantime. *But it is nonsense to say that I wonder at the existence of the world, because I cannot imagine it not existing.* I could of course wonder at the world round me being as it is. If for instance I had this experience while looking into the blue sky, I could wonder at the sky being blue as opposed to the case when it's clouded. I am wondering at the sky being whatever it is.[7]

In his reading of the *Theaetetus*, Heidegger imagines lying in the meadow, seeing the blue of the sky, and hearing the singing of the lark; in this context he wonders at the simplest, most inconspicuous fact, *that things are*. Similarly, on a fine summer day, while looking at the blue sky, Wittgenstein is struck by how extraordinary it is that the world should exist. But his short description of wonder is entangled with a worry about its expression; he quickly identifies its paradoxical character. It makes sense, he says, to wonder at specific things, having particular qualities, because I can imagine what it would be like for these things to be absent or not possess these particular qualities. I can wonder at the existence of a house that I had good reason to assume had been demolished; I can wonder at the sky being blue, given that I am in London where the sky is usually grey. But what would it mean to wonder at the fact that anything exists, at the existence of the world as such? Both the term 'wonder' and the term 'existence' are misused in this context.[8]

Like with the kind of wonder previously discussed, Wittgenstein's wonder differs from the wonder at something unusual. If this wonder were directed at something unusual (such as a dog larger than any one has seen before), there would be no problem of expression. But in the case he describes, what he wonders at is *that* things *are*, not *how* they are. Again, 'that things are' does not mean the sum total of existing things, or the existence of the universe. Rather, it concerns the dimension of intelligibility, the fact that entities appear to us in the first place. This is why Wittgenstein remarks that 'the right expression in language for the miracle of the existence of the world, though it is not any proposition in language, is the existence of language itself'.[9] I take this to mean that Wittgenstein wonders at the fact that the world is present to us, that its existence and the existence of language are equiprimordial. He characterizes this as a miracle. He had previously characterized this as the mystical: it is not how things are in the world that is mystical, but that it is.[10]

Wittgenstein worries that our expressions about this paradoxical miracle – that anything is intelligible in the first place – are themselves unintelligible. He considers propositions in language unfit for the task: 'all we can say about the absolute miraculous remains nonsense'.[11] Wittgenstein was not a logical positivist, but it is hard not to assume that the reason why no proposition in language would work to express the miraculous character of the existence of the world is that he takes the primary function of a proposition to be the description of facts, of states of affairs that can be either true or false. Since one cannot envisage our object of wonder as non-existent, the bipolarity of a proposition (the requirement for it to be either true or false) collapses. Another related angle from which

Wittgenstein articulates the problem – that any expression of wonder at the world's existence would lead to nonsense – is that the astonishment that anything exists cannot be framed as a question and lacks an answer.

Wittgenstein's association of the produced nonsense with the inability to imagine the possibility of something not being the case risks reducing this experience to either a cognitive deficiency (the failure to imagine) or a linguistic limitation (the failure to articulate). While Wittgenstein employs St. Augustine's words to convey a more sympathetic stance towards the nonsense that arises, strongly suggesting that something significant and valuable occurs in such encounters, his characterization of such expressions as nonsensical leaves open the question of whether the paradoxical nature of wonder and anxiety, as described in this book, arises from the failure of having clarity about our grammar – an inherent blind spot in our language that leads to the sense that we are running up against the limits of language. Instead, neither Heidegger nor Kierkegaard seems to be troubled by these issues. Why?

5.2 'The paradox is the wonder'

Because Wittgenstein was aware of the complexities of such encounters and took the ethico-religious dimension of the human life very seriously, he is not dismissive of these encounters and the philosophers who examine them. But other philosophers who have been inspired by his work have not been as charitable. The idea that all paradoxical expressions about 'nothing' (along with all statements of metaphysics) are a case of misuse of language and a failure to draw the right distinctions is the main point of Rudolf Carnap's famous criticism of Heidegger's discussion on 'nothing'. In 'The Elimination of Metaphysics through the Logical Analysis of Language', Carnap argues that Heidegger has not drawn the right distinctions and ends up using the concept of the nothing in different logical roles than the ones it belongs to. Given that 'nothing' is not 'something', but is, Carnap thinks, primarily an extreme case of negation, we should drop any talk about 'nothing' that misuses it as a something, or, if we insist, we should be prepared to get nonsensical statements as a result.

However, whereas in most cases nonsense is, for Carnap, a result of confusion on the part of the person who violates the rules of syntax, Carnap is perplexed by the fact that Heidegger seems to violate logical syntax *knowingly*.[12] He attributes this to Heidegger's artistic attitude or intention.[13] But when Heidegger writes that an encounter with nothing violates logic, he uses inverted commas around the term: it is not logic as such that is challenged but a scientistic kind of logic, like the one Carnap puts forward. Instead of something strange about Heidegger's intention,[14] there is something strange about the encounters themselves that invites not only linguistic innovation but also a broadening of how we understand language's function in the first place.

Heidegger addresses the issue of paradoxicality in his discussion of anxiety as an encounter with nothing: talking about the nothing assumes the form of talking about something and posits 'nothing' as a being – 'nothing "is" such and such' we may want to say when, for example, we discuss the objectlessness of anxiety. This makes questions and answers in regard to the nothing 'inherently absurd'.[15] But Heidegger thinks that this paradoxicality results in a concern that we produce nonsense when we take the exemplar of language and logic to be scientific language and logic. In that case, logic and language are considered to be valid only insofar as they are directed to specific entities. This is not a reproach against science; scientific discourse *must* deal with entities by definition, as entities are its objects of investigation. Science is concerned with entities in an 'exceptional' way, it has to enquire, determine and ground.[16] The problem arises when we take all discourse to be scientific discourse.[17] This leaves no space for a perspective that does not focus on entities: 'the nothing – what else can it be for science but an outrage and a phantasm?',[18] Heidegger asks.

When we attempt to apply the same approach to all forms of thinking, we run the risk of misunderstanding the unique requirements of different objects of investigation. Heidegger gives the example of how mathematics and history differ in terms of the kind of rigor they involve. Demanding mathematical precision in the study of history, for instance, reflects a misunderstanding of the nature of rigor in historical enquiry.[19] Thus if, as discussed earlier, the object of philosophy is the 'there is' itself, then it cannot but concern itself with 'nothing' and may require a language that appears paradoxical at times.[20]

The paradox inherent in these encounters does not stem from flaws in our notation or the confusion of philosophers who assign the wrong logical roles to certain words. Rather, it is an expression of our fundamental condition, namely, that although we are entities in the midst of entities, we also have access to a certain 'beyond' of these entities. We have access to the fact *that they are* in the first place. When the paradox of the encounter with nothing is thematized as illogical, unscientific or nonsensical, and viewed as a problem in need of resolution, it is because our view of language is limited to the perspective of entities. The problem, then, is not that there is a difficulty of expression but rather that *we reduce* this difficulty to a violation of rules of language. In the Carnapian picture, there is an agent who contemplates the world and who can reach a true understanding of the world by correctly applying logic and language. In the Carnapian picture, logic and language serve as tools for representing the world, rather than being seen as intrinsic conditions and expressions of our existence in the world. But as Wittgenstein himself wrote a few years later, the uses of language are countless,[21] and various dimensions of our human lives invite us to explore different possibilities that language offers. Language can be also used for representation, but empirical observations are only *one* dimension of language. Imposing this as a criterion for all uses of language cannot but lead to and stem from a failure to take certain aspects of the human life seriously and a failure to understand the phenomenon of language correctly.

In contrast, for Kierkegaard and Heidegger, understanding of ourselves, of the world and of others cannot be achieved without the appropriate mood. In *The Concept of Anxiety* Kierkegaard (as Vigilius) searches for the right mood for examining original sin, and anxiety is described as a preparatory state for philosophizing. In *The Fundamental Concepts of Metaphysics*, Heidegger distinguishes between concepts that function as determinative representations and the concepts of philosophy or metaphysics. While some concepts represent objects that stand directly before us – such as a house or a lectern – and can be described determinately, other concepts, such as 'the world as a whole', cannot be comprehended without being gripped by them (Ergriffen). This occurs within a mood, rather than through a detached Cartesian cogito.

Similarly, Kierkegaard employs yet another paradoxical statement to express the idea that what we discover in this peculiar wonder does not belong to the realm of understanding, but, rather, to wonder itself. As he puts it, 'the discovery, if it be put it this way, does not belong to the understanding but to the paradox,[22] and 'the understanding has not discovered this; on the contrary, it was the paradox that ushered the understanding to the wonder stool'.[23] His point is that we must not attempt to separate the affective state from understanding. It is not a sequential process where we first contemplate that the world *is*, then experience wonder or anxiety as a result, followed by an attempt to articulate it in words, only to fail in the end. Wonder is not caused by framing the encounter as a paradox, where if one were to find different words or a different way to comprehend the experience, the experience itself would vanish into thin air. These misconceptions view these sudden moods as encounters with the limits of our notation, akin to a logical contradiction. Rather wonder and anxiety are the way we understand something about who we are, hence Kierkegaard writes that the paradox *is* the wonder.

Prioritizing an encounter (moods as a mode of understanding) emphasizes a strong sense of passivity. Emphasizing the primacy of an encounter like wonder or anxiety over the cognitive activity of logical reflection underscores the essential passivity with which we encounter the fact of our existence and the existence of the world.[24] To return to the initial question whether drawing the right distinctions, discarding the term 'nothing' when it creates paradoxes and substituting it with other words would dissolve such encounters, the answer is 'no'. The difficulty of expression and the generation of paradox are intrinsic to the encounter itself: the paradoxicality tells us something about how we ordinarily live our lives in the midst of entities, arises as a result of the fact that this ordinary mode is unavailable or challenged, and constitutes a *form* of understanding rather than its breakdown.

6

After anxiety and wonder

What it means to fulfil our existence and how a human life is best lived is far from clear. We may have biological needs and instincts, cultural standards and social guidelines, but how we understand these, what meaning or significance we assign to them, cannot itself be resolved through a further appeal to biology, psychology or anthropology. As discussed earlier, it is because human existence is an open question that Socrates feels that he must concentrate all his time and thought towards knowing himself.

In this book, I have looked at anxiety and wonder as experiences through which what it means to be human arises as an issue for us. As we live life in the midst of entities, we often become absorbed in the local contexts of meaning, or we narrow our focus to entities and use the public interpretations[1] available to relate to those and to ourselves (qua entities). Anxiety and wonder suspend this everyday forgetfulness and turn the human existence into a question: who we are and what we are for become worthy of interrogation as our actual lives with entities are interrupted and as we are profoundly moved by something that is not itself an entity. As discussed, what speaks in this anxious wonder are not the particulars of one's individual life, or of the culture one is a member of, but a more general trait of human existence that may go unnoticed or neglected. That in the face of which we experience an anxious wonder is the simple yet mysterious fact that things appear to us in the first place and that we are sense-makers. If this simple and seemingly empty fact can have a profound and passionate grip on us, throwing us out of our ordinary life and moods and into the question of existence as such, what does this tell us about being human and its possibilities?

Indeed, an important point of the book has been that wonder and anxiety do not just present our existence as a problem. They are neither cases of a sceptical threat that makes us anxious nor cases of a constant questioning or wonderment at everything. They also offer an answer, or, rather, a direction. Instead of only leaving us with an undoing of what we knew about the human existence, a mere question mark, they point towards a trait that defines us, a capacity we have and we are called to exercise. Drawing upon Heidegger's and Kierkegaard's dynamic reading of the human existence, I approached this as a capacity for openness and associated it with our ability and task to make sense, to open possibilities of meaning. The two functions of wonder and anxiety, that they show the human existence as a question and that they point towards its openness, are interlinked given that we could not be open without being open-ended.[2] Being open is possible because we are ontologically suspended, instances of finite becoming with no definite direction, or predetermined *telos*, unlike the being of a table-under-construction and unlike the being of God, to return to Sheehan's helpful analogies. Our *telos* is, paradoxically speaking, the task to find a home in our ontological suspension, to recognize its creative potential. 'Ontologically [human existence] is going nowhere because it always already is where it is supposed to be.'[3] But this seemingly small task, to recognize what is already available to us, is also the most difficult because, as Kierkegaard repeatedly points out, the human condition is characterized by a structural ambivalence towards openness and possibility.

Keeping alive the tension between open-endedness and openness means recognizing that insofar as things are present to us, we have a *task* to make them present, and insofar as we are in a world, we have a task to form worlds, by exercising the unique sense-making capacity that we have. Such a life of making present or world-forming should not be confused with what is commonly referred to as an intellectual life or a life of questioning and doubting public interpretations. Jan Patočka warns against this temptation. He highlights a distinction that Plato was deeply concerned with: the difference between what Patočka calls the 'spiritual person' (such as Socrates) and the 'person of intelligence' or 'intellectual' (such as Protagoras).[4] Being an intellectual and engaging in critical thinking against prevailing public opinions does not guarantee a view of the world that recognizes its openness. Relatedly, Wittgenstein accuses certain intellectuals ('philosophers') of 'a loss of problems':

> Some philosophers (or whatever you like to call them) suffer from what may be called 'loss of problems'. Then everything seems quite simple to them, no deep problems seem to exist anymore, the world becomes broad and flat and loses all depth, and what they write becomes immeasurably shallow and trivial. Russell and H.G. Wells suffer from this.[5]

Regardless of whether Wittgenstein is right in his judgment about Russell and Wells, neither of them could ever be accused of not having a rational perspective towards the world or not seeking knowledge. But a life that is open to our being-possible is not just a life of doubt or critical thinking, but it is a life 'to which that from whence it came and whither it again departs continually speaks'.[6] It is a life that sustains the wonder at the mysterious fact that things are present to us. This point links back to my discussion in Chapter 4, where I distinguished the activity of philosophizing from an activity of mere critical thinking or conceptual analysis. Instead, as the natural dwelling of the human existence, philosophy must first and foremost manifest an ability to sustain the question of the human existence, to wonder at the fact that things are present to us in the first place.[7] Patočka also connects the spiritual person with the activity of philosophizing and, relatedly, disconnects the figure of the intellectual person from the figure of the philosopher; philosophizing is an exposure to the negative, to the 'strange wonderment of our situation – that we are at all and that the world is – [and] that this is not self-evident'.[8] When Heidegger defines the human existence as one for which its own being is an issue for it, he crucially adds the phrase 'in its Being'.[9] I take this to mean that our defining trait is not merely that we can *think* about our role in the world, that we are rational animals that can theorize about our place in the universe, but that the way we organize our lives, the way we make sense of things around us is motivated – even when we do not realize it – by a broader concern about our life as a whole, by the fact that the world matters. Once again, this mattering is possible to the extent that human existence has no definite direction, and has been given to us in finitude, with no obvious reason.

Kierkegaard introduces the term 'spiritlessness' to describe an existence that relies solely on the categories of nature and culture to understand itself. The problem is not that one relies on *certain* categories of nature and culture (say the most naïve or uncritical ones); rather, the problem of spiritlessness arises when we regard ourselves *only* as products of nature and culture. In doing so, we fail to recognize our openness. As (Kierkegaard's pseudonym) Vigilius Haufniensis puts it in *The Concept of Anxiety*, '[t]he lostness of spiritlessness, as well as its security, consists in its understanding nothing spiritually and comprehending nothing as a task' (1980, 95). This is the lack of depth that Wittgenstein warns against: a view of one's life as unproblematic, of one's existence as involving no task (apart from the ordinary tasks in one's individual or social life). Kierkegaard also connects this spiritlessness with a tendency to boast about not having ever been in anxiety, not having experienced the unsettling attunements that I have discussed in this book.

> If [...] the speaker maintains the great thing about him is that he has never been in anxiety, I will gladly provide him with my explanation: that it is because he's very spiritless.[10]

Given that an attitude of openness encompasses a receptiveness to such emotional states, the effort required to maintain our openness aligns with the effort needed to cultivate conditions conducive to wonder and anxiety.[11] Hence, Haufniensis remarks that 'to learn what it is to be in anxiety [...] is an adventure that every human being must go through',[12] and Heidegger speaks of a 'preservation of the wondrous'[13] and of making oneself 'ready for the unconditional necessity that holds sway in [wonder]'.[14]

How do we prepare ourselves for anxiety and wonder? Learning to be in anxiety and wonder must mean taking a distance from their ordinary forms. The main reason for this is that, as discussed previously, ordinary forms of anxiety and wonder mistake entities for the only source of significance and fail to go beyond them. As Haufniensis remarks, passing through 'the anxiety of the possible' will make 'anxiety about men and finitudes' lose its significance: '[H]e who passes through the anxiety of the possible is educated to have no anxiety, not because he can escape the terrible things of life but because these always become weak by comparison with those of possibility.'[15] In anxiety we get a taste of our infinitude – our ability to transcend the actuality of our condition and orientate our life towards possibility. Similarly, preparing to be gripped by 'the wonder of all wonders' cannot but involve a certain distance from ordinary kinds of wonder, as 'this wonder no longer adheres to this or that, from which it could still explain the unusualness of the usual and thereby could dispel its unusualness and turn it into something ordinary'.[16] By 'distance' one should not hear an urge to eliminate ordinary kinds of wonder, but rather a recognition that those sources of wonder (entities) reflect only a part of our existence rather than the whole picture.

Moreover, preparing for wonder and preparing for anxiety overlap. Recognizing their overlap – feeling the nearness of wonder when we are in anxiety and the nearness of anxiety when we are in wonder – means that we identify correctly what is at stake, namely we recognize that what lights up in these attunements is our openness, an openness that becomes available because of our open-endedness. This anxious wonder manifests a call towards our 'ownmost potentiality-for-being', our 'being-free'[17]: our freedom lies in our openness and our openness is exercised insofar as we form worlds and we relate to entities meaningfully. Relatedly, Haufniensis writes that 'whoever is educated by anxiety is educated by possibility, and only he who was educated by possibility is educated according to his infinitude',[18] and when Heidegger speaks of a preparation for anxiety, he highlights the importance of learning to experience being (the givenness of meaning) in the nothing.[19] This is not about finding the silver lining or perceiving the good consequences of something bad. It is not about recognizing potential existential benefits of something painful. Rather, it is about recognizing in the encounter with nothing our distinct capacity to be moved by something that is not itself a being.[20] In Heideggers passionate words:

> Readiness for anxiety is a Yes to assuming a stance that fulfils the highest claim, a claim that is made upon the human essence alone. Of all beings, only the human being, called upon by the voice of being, experiences the wonder of all wonders: that beings are. [...] The lucid courage for essential

anxiety assures us the enigmatic possibility of experiencing being. For close by essential anxiety as the horror of the abyss dwells awe.[21]

Externally, a life that exercises openness and is directed to possibility may not look very different from a spiritless life. These lives may appear as the lives of 'writers like other writers, teachers like other teachers,'[22] of individuals fulfilling their practical identities. This is because this kind of life is not easily defined by specific observable facts, traits or activities. However, the orientation of their lives is shifted, and the overall tone is different. Wittgenstein makes a similar point in his *Tractatus Logico-Philosophicus* when he suggests that although the world of a happy person must be an altogether different world from the world of the unhappy person, it is impossible to reduce this to specific facts that are different.[23] This difficulty of externally defining the life of openness mirrors the difficulty of defining objectless moods. As Heidegger remarks, the voice of what speaks to us in such strange moods is 'a silent voice,'[24] a voice that can easily escape our notice, requiring attentiveness and receptivity. It is my hope that this book has contributed to that.

NOTES

Chapter 1

1   I will mostly use the terms 'mood', 'affect', 'feeling' and 'emotion'
    interchangeably, despite a tradition in philosophy to treat moods as
    more holistic, background and global affective states; indeed Heidegger's
    own German word for mood, 'Befindlichkeit', points to this background,
    long-term character. 'Befindlichkeit' can be translated as so-findingness.
    In German, we ask how someone is by asking 'Wie befinden Sie
    sich?', 'How do you find yourself?'. This, for Heidegger, shows that
    moods (alongside understanding and discourse) are equiprimordial
    determinants of our being-in-the-world, and that our lives are always
    already directed, situated and attuned, prior to any specific feelings
    that may arise. However, although it is important to keep in mind that
    our affective life can have this background character, Heidegger never
    explicitly distinguishes between 'mood' and 'emotion'. The reason for
    that is that the boundaries between the background mood and the
    focused emotion are not clear-cut. For instance, he suggests that the
    emotion of fear can also be called a mood if we think of it as fearfulness.
    See M. Heidegger, *Being and Time,* trans. J. Macquarrie and E. Robinson
    (New York: Harper & Row, 1962), 181–2, 142. Hereafter abbreviated
    as B&T. Page references will be given in the form (B&T xx, yy) where
    the first page number refers to the English Macquarrie and Robinson
    translation and the second to the Niemeyer pagination, which is
    included in the margins of English translations.
       Or, to use Matthew Ratcliffe's example, the love for one's child can
    be both a world-changing background state and a specified emotion
    at the same time, depending on how we look at it. Some moods, like
    the ones I discuss in this book, have the added feature of revealing
    something about our human condition, rather than just constituting

it. But given that the distinction between 'moods' and 'feelings' / 'emotions' is not always clear-cut, a 'feeling' or an 'emotion' can also be said to do that. What matters for my purposes, is that I conceive of these affective experiences as all-encompassing, enveloping and as disruptive of our usual affective states, without being tied to any worldly change. For a synopsis of the complexities around the distinction between moods, feelings and emotions see M. Ratcliffe, 'Why Mood Matters', in *The Cambridge Companion to Heidegger's Being and Time*, ed. M. Wrathall (Cambridge: Cambridge University Press, 2013), 157–76.

2   As Heidegger puts it when he discusses such a mood through the case of anxiety, they do not even 'have any need for darkness, in which it is commonly easier for one to feel uncanny'. See B&T 234, 189.

3   We also use these two terms – anxiety and wonder – to refer to affects that are *about something* definite; earlier I mentioned an example of anxiety in this first category of revelatory moods (feeling anxious in the prospect of one's fiftieth birthday), and similarly we can think of all those cases where wonder is directed at something definite in the world (we wonder at someone's dancing skills, at a new scientific discovery, at the stars).

4   B&T 231, 186.

5   A psychological way to think about this is that when one misses a loved one, this loved one is present in their absence.

6   J. Patočka, 'The Spiritual Person and the Intellectual', in *Care for the Soul: The Selected Writings of Jan Patočka*, ed. I. Chvatic and E. Plunkett (London: Bloomsbury, 2022), 294–305, 298.

7   'That in the face of which one has anxiety is Being-in-the-World as such', as Heidegger puts it in his account of anxiety. B&T 230, 186.

8   T. Sheehan, 'Dasein', in *A Companion to Heidegger*, ed. H. L. Dreyfus and M. A. Wrathall (Oxford: Blackwell Publishing, 2005), 200.

9   To put it differently, all the specific worlds rest on the transcendental condition for meaning. This must be a priori given for any specific world (like the above) to occur in the first place, in order for anything to appear to us in the first place.

10 Heidegger describes this capacity as 'being-possible' and 'world-formation'. World-forming and being possible are two ways to describe the same structural feature of the human existence, an active capacity to open worlds, to move beyond what is actual towards what is possible. See B&T, 183. See also M. Heidegger, *The Fundamental Concepts of Metaphysics* (Bloomington: Indiana University Press, 1995), 285.

11 Such an interpretation aligns more closely with the experience of absurdity portrayed by the Sartrean character Roquentin, where the world's limitless potentiality induces nausea. See J.-P. Sartre, *Nausea* (London: Penguin Books, 1963). The description of the mood of nausea was first introduced by Levinas to describe an experience that is, I think, closer to what Heidegger describes than to what Sartre describes. It is an experience of a sudden awareness of the 'there is', the 'il y a' -that things are in the first place. See E. Levinas, *On Escape*, trans. B. Bergo (Stanford, California: Stanford University Press, 2003).

12 Heidegger B&T, 183, 144.

13 This is how Kierkegaard puts it. See S. Kierkegaard, *The Concept of Anxiety* (Princeton: Princeton University Press, 1980). Heidegger also speaks of a similar tendency as a tendency to flee in the face of our human existence as a whole. See B&T, 229, 184.

14 Psychopathology is the study of mental disorders and is central to psychiatry, psychology, and various schools of psychotherapy. Its most basic assumption is that the human mind (or psyche) can, in some cases, be dysfunctional or in a state of disorder, which manifests itself in symptoms. This assumption underlies the standard manuals for psychiatric diagnosis, such as ICD and DSM. It is because of this underlying assumption that, in Chapter 2, I refer to psychopathology in terms of discourse or narrative.

15 'The concept of anxiety is almost never treated in psychology, therefore I must point out that it is altogether different from fear and similar concepts that refer to something definite, whereas anxiety is freedom's actuality as the possibility of possibility'. Kierkegaard, *The Concept of Anxiety*, 42.

16 Even if he restricts the acknowledgement of his debt to him to footnotes, two in *Being and Time* and one in *The Fundamental Concepts of Metaphysics*.

17 See Kierkegaard, *The Concept of Anxiety*, 44; M. Heidegger, *Pathmarks* (Cambridge: Cambridge University Press, 1998), 233; M. Heidegger, *Basic Questions of Philosophy: Selected 'Problems' of 'Logic'* (Bloomington: Indiana University Press, 1994), 146. Drawing from their ideas in a way that remains close to the topic per se, and does not deviate too much into the exegetical problems related to each thinker's work, meant that I have had to sacrifice some of the conceptual complexity in the following ways: I generally understand Heidegger's term 'Being' in terms of the givenness of meaning, or meaningfulness. I also translate Heidegger's *'Dasein'* with the simpler 'human existence', although I still understand 'human existence' as a dynamic openness to possibility. For a discussion on the overlap between Heidegger's concept of Being (*Sein*) and the concept of meaningfulness, see T. Sheehan, 'What if Heidegger were a Phenomenologist?', in *The Cambridge Companion to Heidegger's Being and Time*, ed. M. Wrathall (Cambridge: Cambridge University Press, 2013), 381–401.

In translating Dasein as human existence I follow Sheehan in M. Heidegger, *Logic: The Question of Truth.* (Studies in Continental Thought), trans. T. Sheehan (Bloomington: Indiana University Press, 2016), xi. In citations that refer to *'Dasein'* I keep the original term and add the above translation in brackets, where appropriate.

18 See Heidegger, *The Fundamental Concepts of Metaphysics*, 285.

19 R. Polt, *Heidegger: An Introduction* (Ithaca, NY: Cornell University Press, 1999), 57.

20 K. Withy, *Heidegger on Being Uncanny* (Cambridge, MA: Harvard University Press, 2015), 71.

21 Kierkegaard, *The Concept of Anxiety,* 85.

22 For a related discussion on continuities and differences between Heidegger and Kierkegaard, see C. Carlisle, 'A Tale of Two Footnotes: Heidegger and the Question of Kierkegaard', in *Heidegger, Authenticity, and the Self: Themes from Division Two of Being and*

Time, ed. D. McManus (London: Routledge, 2015), and D. Magurshak, 'The Concept of Anxiety: The Keystone of the Kierkegaard-Heidegger Relationship', in *International Kierkegaard Commentary: The Concept of Anxiety*, Volume 8, ed. Robert Perkins (Macon, GA: Mercer University Press, 1985), 167–95.

23 B&T, 30, 10.

24 See Heidegger, 'What Is Metaphysics?', in *Basic Writings*, ed. and trans. D.F. Krell (London: Routledge, 2011), 41–57, 55–6. Hereafter abbreviated as WIM.

25 Kierkegaard often wrote under pseudonyms and used those pseudonyms to express or try out different voices. The question how to understand and deal with his use of pseudonyms is largely controversial and differs from case to case. In the case of the two works I discuss, although he writes under two different pseudonyms, Vigilius Haufniensis and Johannes Climacus, given the continuity of the works, I often refer to ideas in those works as coming from Kierkegaard himself. When I use a quote or a specific terminology from the specific work, then I usually refer to the pseudonym.

26 Unlike despair that can be overcome by faith, anxiety becomes educative through faith. This is why Vigilius writes that Christ, a figure greater than the knight of faith, 'was anxious unto death'. See Kierkegaard, *The Concept of Anxiety*, 155.

27 St. Mulhall, *Philosophical Myths of the Fall* (London and Princeton: Princeton University Press, 2005), 49.

28 For a discussion on the profound influence that early Christian thinking (especially St Paul) has had on Heidegger's *Being and Time* and his account of the human existence (the concept of '*Dasein*'), see T. Sheehan, 'Heidegger's "Introduction to the Phenomenology of Religion", 1920–21', in *A Companion to Martin Heidegger's Being and Time*, ed. J.J. Kockelmans (Washington, D.C.: Center for Advanced Research in Phenomenology & University Press of America, 1986), 40–62.

Chapter 2

1 G. Glas, 'Anxiety-Animal Reactions and the Embodiment of Meaning', in *Nature and Narrative: An Introduction to the New Philosophy of Psychiatry*, ed. B. Fulford, K. Morris, J. Sadler and G. Stanghellini (Oxford: Oxford University Press, 2003), 231–49, 231.

2 See Kierkegaard, *The Concept of Anxiety*, 162 and 42, respectively.

3 See, for example, WIM, 50; Kierkegaard, *The Concept of Anxiety*, 42.

4 B&T, 230.

5 See Heidegger, WIM.

6 'Flee away from anxiety [man] cannot, for he loves it', Kierkegaard, *The Concept of Anxiety*, 44.

7 'It is 'a shrinking back before… that is surely not any sort of flight but rather a kind of bewildered calm', WIM, 51.

8 WIM, 54.

9 Matthew Ratcliffe, for example, reproaches Heidegger for not having drawn the appropriate distinctions that would allow for a conversation with psychiatrists and psychologists, and the kinds of experience that 'people report' when suffering from anxiety or depression. See Ratcliffe, *Why Mood Matters*, 171–2.

10 The versions of the scientific study of anxiety (including neurobiology, psychology, psychopharmacology, psychiatry) are summarized by Gerrit Glas:

> **(1)** A Darwinian, ethological tradition in which anxiety is seen as a universal, biologically anchored survival response, which has become sensitive to a range of environmental cues via conditioning and other learning processes; generally speaking, most neurobiological research fits in this tradition, which has been very influential in psychopharmacology.

(2) A strong empiricist, initially mainly behaviorist research
tradition, which views anxiety as a theoretical term denoting
observable behavior that is considered to be the expression
of activation of different neural and/or behavioral systems
[…] Within this tradition anxiety is not by definition a
unite phenomenon, but composed of building blocks like
physiological symptoms, behavior manifestations and verbal
behavior. Most animal research is performed within this
framework […]

(3) A cognitive research tradition which focuses on anxiety
as inner experience, influenced by expectancies, (mis)
interpretations, (biased) attention, and cognitive schemes […].

These three traditions are not mutually exclusive but share their
background assumptions. As Glas further remarks: 'According to
contemporary leading psychologists and cognitive neuroscientists
these traditions do not exclude one another [and] their interactions
should be placed against the background of the perennial question
whether emotions are natural kinds or the result of environmental
influences'. See G. Glas, 'An Enactive Approach to Anxiety and
Anxiety Disorders', *Philosophy, Psychiatry, & Psychology* 27, no. 1
(2020): 35–50, 40.

11 Kierkegaard, *The Concept of Anxiety*, 42.

12 For example, in *The Fundamental Concepts of Metaphysics* Heidegger
asks his students to refrain from thinking of boredom as an observable
object in the stream of consciousness (90). Similarly, he invites us
to treat distress as sometimes distinct from what is 'deficient […]
miserable and lamentable' or from what arises 'psychically in man
as 'lived experience' and to think of it, instead, as a characteristic of
human existence. See Heidegger, *Basic Questions of Philosophy*, 133.

13 Heidegger, *Pathmarks*, 234.

14 See Kierkegaard, *The Concept of Anxiety*, 43; see also Heidegger,
WIM, 51.

15 Heidegger suggests that only anxiety reveals the nothing directly.
Although to the best of my knowledge he does not ever juxtapose

wonder to anxiety (in contrast, he often brings them together, as I discuss later), he juxtaposes anxiety to boredom on the basis that the latter does not reveal the nothing. For example, he writes: 'Dasein is now merely suspended among beings and their telling refusal of themselves as a whole. The emptiness is not a hole between things that are filled, but concerns beings as a whole and yet is not the Nothing.' Heidegger, *The Fundamental Concepts of Metaphysics*, 140. I find it puzzling why Heidegger excludes boredom from attunements that open us onto the nothing, given that he takes boredom to open us to the fundamental question of metaphysics ('why are there beings at all, rather than nothing?'). I think that a more refined way of putting it would be more appropriate, for example, that boredom does not open us onto the nothing *directly*, and that only anxiety does that.

16 The DSM-5 uses this distinction from fear to define anxiety disorder as follows: 'anxiety disorders include disorders that share features of excessive fear and anxiety and related behavioral disturbances. Fear is the emotional response to real or perceived imminent threat, whereas anxiety is anticipation of future threat. Obviously, these two states overlap, but they also differ, with fear more often associated with surges of autonomic arousal necessary for fight or flight, thoughts of immediate danger, and escape behaviors, and anxiety more often associated with muscle tension and vigilance in preparation for future danger and cautious or avoidant behaviors. Sometimes the level of fear or anxiety is reduced by pervasive avoidance behaviors. Panic attacks feature prominently within the anxiety disorders as a particular type of fear response. Panic attacks are not limited to anxiety disorders but rather can be seen in other mental disorders as well.' American Psychiatric Association, *American Psychiatric Association: Diagnostic and Statistical Manual of Mental Disorders*, fifth edn (Arlington, VA: American Psychiatric Association, 2013), 189.

17 My aim is not primarily exegetical; hence I do not offer a detailed investigation of the conceptual changes in Freud's work on anxiety.

18 Kierkegaard links this to freedom: 'anxiety is freedom's actuality as the possibility of possibility'. See *The Concept of Anxiety*, 42.

19 S. Freud, *Introductory Lectures on Psycho-Analysis*, Standard Edition 16 (London: Hogarth Press, 1916–1917), 15–16, 393. Hereafter the Standard Edition will be abbreviated as SE. All references to Freud are to it, unless otherwise specified.

20 'Anxiety appears as the reaction to the felt loss of the objects and we are at once reminded of the fact that castration anxiety too is a fear of being separated from a highly valued object and that the earliest anxiety of all – in the primal anxiety of birth – is brought about on the occasion of a separation from the mother.' S. Freud, *Inhibitions, Symptoms and Anxiety*. SE 20 (London: Hogarth Press, 1925–1926), 137.

21 The central role of the loss of the mother – if it is not reduced to a highly valued object – could also point to the direction that I am interested in, since the mother is not just an important object of attachment but the relationship through which the 'as a whole', the conditions for making sense, is given. The bond between mother (or the primal caretaker) and child is, we could say, where the human being first experiences meaningfulness. Wilfred Bion's work bears, in some respects, on that connection. For a discussion on how Bion's work could accommodate some of the ontological aspects of anxiety, see C. Mawson, *Psychoanalysis and Anxiety: From Knowing to Being* (London: Routledge, 2019).

22 See SE 20, 85.

23 In the Addenda of *Inhibitions, Symptoms, Anxiety* Freud highlights that the dangers signalled by anxiety are dangers to the ego, not a threat to life, hence birth cannot be a danger in that sense; for the same reason, death or the annihilation of life cannot be either, given that 'nothing resembling death can ever have been experienced' and 'the unconscious seems to contain nothing that could give any content to our concept of the annihilation of life'. SE 20, 129.

24 SE 20, 152.

25 Whether aware or unaware of it, when Freud recognizes the unique character of this primordial dimension of anxiety in humans, he touches on the fact that anxiety is a structural feature of the human existence. Mawson makes a similar point in *Psychoanalysis and Anxiety*, xxvi.

26 SE 20, 155.

27 Ibid.

28 SE 20, 155–6.

29 SE 20, 156.

30 SE 20, 164–5.

31 Freud writes: 'When, in analysis, we have given the ego assistance which is able to put it in a position to lift its repressions, it recovers its power over the repressed id and can allow the instinctual impulses to run their course as though the old situations of danger no longer existed. What we can do in this way tallies with what can be achieved in other fields of medicine; for as a rule our therapy must be content with bringing about more quickly, more reliably and with less expenditure of energy than would otherwise be the case the good result which in favourable circumstances would have occurred of itself', SE 20, 154.

32 SE 16, 394.

33 SE 16, 394, my emphasis.

34 See S. Freud, *Studies on Hysteria*. SE 2 (London: Hogarth Press, 1893–1895), 181.

35 This adaptation model of the human subject finds its clearest expression in ego psychology.

36 This is how Samuel Arbiser summarizes Freud's ideas on anxiety, as deriving from his recognition of a tension between: '[T]he object of psychoanalysis is the inevitable suffering derived from the circumstances and events of man's life as it develops in a socio-cultural environment. This would be consistent with the assertion that we share with the animal world a significant part of the generation of affects which, in *Homo sapiens*, would be the matrix upon which the historical (non-instinctive) part of affective life, now dependent on the learning process in the family and the socio-cultural milieu, is inserted.' S. Arbiser, 'An Unexpected Clinical Experience: Rethinking Affects', in *On Freud's 'Inhibitions, Symptoms and Anxiety'*, ed. S. Arbiser and J. Schneider (London: Karnac Books, 2013), 415–35, 417.

37 'The well-known phenomenon of animals fleeing in terror moments before a natural disaster […] comes to mind. In the same way that the newborn human infant loses its innate ability to swim after a few weeks of extra-uterine life, a large part of the intrinsic affects in the animal world (at the service of self-healing, protection from predators and from natural contingencies) are relinquished in the process of the humanisation.' Ibid., 432.

38 Charles Shepherdson makes the same point: 'The adaptive account in which anxiety functions properly when it is realistic and serves to identify a real danger, and improperly when it arises from an internal conflict, does not really distinguish between anxiety and fear. If we stay with the model of self-preservation, anxiety should resolve itself into fear, and the distinction between the two should disappear when the organism is functioning properly.' In R. Harari, *Lacan's Seminar on 'Anxiety': An Introduction* (New York: Other Press, 2001), lvii.

39 Lacan remarks: 'If the ego is the locus of the signal, then the signal isn't given for the ego. This is quite clear.' In remarking this, Lacan reads Freud's account much more generously than I do; in fact, he thinks Freud would agree with him. Lacan characterizes the whole seminar on anxiety as a reading of Freud. Whether his interpretations are indeed close to what Freud meant also depends on what it means to interpret a text, how creative this process is meant to be. If it is meant to be creative, then we could say that Lacan brings out what is repressed in Freud, his connection to philosophy. See J. Lacan, *Anxiety. The Seminar: Book 10*, trans. A.R. Price, ed. J.-A. Miller (Cambridge: Polity Press, 2014), 153.

40 Ibid., 18.

41 Ibid.

42 Lacan describes this scene as follows:

> Already, just in the exemplary little image with which the demonstration of the mirror stage begins, the moment that is said to be jubilatory when the child, grasping himself in the inaugural experience of recognition in the mirror, comes to terms with himself as a totality functioning as such in his specular

image, haven't I always insisted on the movement that the infant makes? This movement is so frequent, constant I'd say, that each and every one of you may have some recollection of it. Namely, he turns round, I noted, to the one supporting him who's there behind him. If we force ourselves to assume the content of the infant's experience and to reconstruct the sense of this movement, we shall say that, with this nutating movement of the head, which turns towards the adult as if to call upon his assent, and then back to the image, he seems to be asking the one supporting him, and who here represents the big Other, to ratify the value of this image. This is nothing, of course, but an indication concerning the inaugural nexus between this relation to the big Other and the advent of the function of the specular image. Ibid., 32.

In Lacan's work the Other (with a capital 'o', also referred to as the big other) stands for the Symbolic, the dimension of symbolization, which significantly overlaps with language. The Other can be the dimension of the signifier, the realm of language and symbolization, or another person insofar as they also bear this dimension of the symbolic.

43 Ibid., 50. There is an interesting, even if limited, overlap here between the fact that in Lacan anxiety reveals the play of desire (the structural role that desire plays in our being-in-the-world) and the fact that for Heidegger anxiety reveals the structure of care (Sorge). See B&T, 227, 183.

44 A helpful way to depict the object *a* as a paradox of unconcealing concealment is a veil placed around an empty place. While hiding it, the veil also draws attention to what it hides (what is not there). But because every concealment is as such an unconcealment of what is concealed – in this case, castration – is also revealed precisely as the object of desire, which Lacan calls object *a*. In the specular image, then, as what embodies the gaze of the other, namely, as object of desire, the function of the object *a* as a concealment of the lack of the phallus ($-\varphi$) is already at play.

45 Lacan, *Anxiety*, 103.

46 In other words, anxiety emerges at the point of a tension between the concealment and unconcealment of castration (of lack). Anxiety concerns the imaginary body (not the real body) and the loss of this imaginary unity/integrity, namely, of castration in the imaginary body. Recall that the specular image, as the way into the construction of the ego, is a case of concealing lack through the image of a harmonious unity, which is, however, an illusion – it is imaginary. Anxiety, for Lacan, is an overflow of internal excitations that cannot be contained by this *imaginary* integrity of the body:

> 'Here we are, then, in a position to reply to the question: when does anxiety emerge? Anxiety emerges when a mechanism makes something appear in the place of what I will call, to make myself understood, a natural place, namely, the place of minus phi ($-\varphi$), which corresponds […] to the place that is occupied […] by the *a* of the object of desire. I say something – you should understand anything whatsoever'. Ibid., 41.

Later on, he gives a name to this 'something-anything whatsoever':

> 'The *Unheimliche* is what appears at the place where the minus phi should be. Indeed, everything starts with imaginary castration, because there is no image of lack, and with good reason. When something does appear there, it is, therefore, if I may put it this way, because lack happens to be lacking'. Ibid., 42.

47 The centrality of the eyes is an interesting common thread here between Freud's reading of Hoffmann's tale in his essay *The Uncanny* and Lacan's example of anxiety in the face of our own gaze. For Lacan, the central role of the eye (gaze) amounts to the centrality of desire, see Lacan, *Anxiety*, 315. Although Lacan refers a few times to Freud's discussion of the uncanny, Freud himself seems to associate the uncanny primarily with fear, rather than anxiety. S. Freud, 'The Uncanny', in *An Infantile Neurosis and Other Works*, SE 17 (London: Hogarth Press, 1917–1919). Commenting on Ernst Jentsch's examples and Hoffmann's tale 'The Sandman', Freud links the uncanny to an interplay between familiarity and unfamiliarity where the unfamiliar is experienced as uncanny because at some stage it was familiar. This stage is an animistic phase in the history of our species and in the history of the individual (in childhood). Hence for Freud the uncanny corresponds to the return of the repressed. See E. Jentsch, 'On the Psychology of the Uncanny', trans. Roy Sellars, *Angelaki: A New Journal in Philosophy, Literature and the Social Sciences* 2, no. 1 (1996): 7–16. See E.T.A. Hoffmann, 'The Sandman', in *The Golden Pot and Other Tales*, trans. Ritchie Robertson (Oxford: Oxford University Press, 1992).

48 See Lacan, *Anxiety*, 53.

49 We see this often in neurotics, how they 'prefer' to develop symptoms, or to repeat the same problematic life choices so as not to deal with the possibilities that could open up if they were free.

50 In more specialist Lacanian terms, the place of imagined castration (what appears as Unheimlich) is man's home. As Lacan puts it, 'the place designated first time as the minus phi by its name – this is what is called the *Heim*. [...] We have here man's home. [...] man finds his home at a point located in the Other that lies beyond the image from which we are fashioned. This place represents the absence where we stand'. Ibid., 47. That man's home is in the absence where we stand means that for humans the *Heim* and the *Unheim* are tightly connected: 'it is the definition of the *unheimlich* to be the *heimlich*. This is what is at stake in the *Heim* which is *Unheim*'. Ibid., 60. As Anneleen Masschelein comments:

> 'According to Lacan, *Heim* as a structural position is the place designated to – ϕ. It represents 'the absence where we are'. This is also the place of man in the realm of the Other, that is, beyond the image. The specular image that we perceive in the place of the Other, which renders our perception of ourselves as subject foreign or uncanny to us, is precisely the phallus that appears where it should be lacking, undoing the castration that is necessary to constitute us as divided subjects'.

A. Masschelein, *The Unconcept: The Freudian Uncanny in Late-Twentieth-Century Theory* (Albany: SUNY Press, 2012), 55.

51 In his discussion of Lacan's concept of *Heim*, Baas brings this out
and argues that Lacan's position is close to that of Heidegger: 'But,
Heidegger specifies, "the outside oneself" ["*hors-de-chez-soi*"]
must be ontologically-existentially conceived as the most originary
phenomenon, in other words, as the most intimate, in such a way,
that in relation to it, what habitually appears as the most familiar,
the most reassuring, the "at home" ["*chez-soi*"] constitutes precisely
the uncanniness of the human existence [*Dasein*]: in anxiety, the "*chez-
soi*" becomes strange and the strange reveals itself as originary, familiar
and intimate. The subject cannot but lose itself there, faint there'. Baas
cited in Masschelein, *The Unconcept*, 169.

52 H.L. Dreyfus, *Being-in-the-World: A Commentary on Heidegger's Being
and Time, Division I* (Cambridge, MA: The MIT Press, 1991), 25.

53 Ibid., 179.

54 Philipse, *Heidegger's Philosophy of Being*, 395.

55 Blattner, *Heidegger's Being and Time*, 139–40.

56 Given the fact that Heidegger also offers more positive descriptions for
anxiety, such as wonder, calm and even joyfulness, these readings must
attribute such positive affects not to anxiety as such but to the fruits of
anxiety, namely, to authenticity. Joy in this case is what is experienced
by the authentic ones when they are hit by anxiety, those who do not
get absorbed in the They (*das Man*). As Denis McManus describes this
view, 'anxiety reveals that the world is – in this sense – meaningless;
in this way, anxiety embodies a 'window on the truth'. This realization
paralyses some of us – the inauthentic – who have 'clung' to such
justifications. But others amongst us do not need the 'pity' that that
fantasy promises. The authentic are 'ready for anxiety' because they
have tied their lives to projects that speak to them and for which
they feel no need of such a justification: anxiety 'neither inhibits nor
bewilders' them'. D. McManus, 'Anxiety, Choice, and Responsibility',
in *Heidegger, Authenticity and the Self: Themes from Division Two of
Being and Time*, ed. D. McManus (London: Routledge, 2015), 163–85,
177. Although Heidegger does connect anxiety to authenticity in
Division 2, I think that restricting anxiety to inauthenticity and
authenticity entails several risks that I want to avoid. First it may entail

a wrong assumption that authenticity is a once-and-for-all achievable state that some humans attain rather than an 'inherently precarious' mode. See T. Staehler, 'How Is a Phenomenology of Fundamental Moods Possible?', *International Journal of Philosophical Studies* 15, no. 3 (2007): 415–33, 419. Second, talk of authenticity in Heidegger's work has often been regarded as politically conservative or dubious, see T.W. Adorno, *The Jargon of Authenticity*, trans. Knut Tarnowski and Frederic Will (Evanston, IL: Northwestern University Press, 1973). Finally, the accounts that McManus summarizes above miss an important and unique point that Heidegger makes about anxiety as an encounter with the fact that there is a world in the first place, the givenness of meaning. Taking seriously this aspect of the encounter with nothing invites us to think of affects such as joy and calm as inherent parts of the experience of anxiety, rather than as external benefits.

57 See B&T, 186, 230–1. Also in 'What is Metaphysics?' we read: 'Anxiety is basically different from fear.' WIM, 50. Yet already this distinction from fear is very different from the distinction drawn by Freud. Whereas in Freud's case, fear is more directly connected to the human as an organism, for Heidegger fear is already a state of mind characteristic of an entity for which its being is an issue, which has concerns and for which things matter. See B&T, 180, 141, and Ratcliffe, *Why Mood Matters*, 163–4.

58 B&T, 187, 231–2.

59 '[I]n anxiety all things and we ourselves sink into indifference. This, however, not in the sense of mere disappearance. Rather, in this very receding things turn toward us'. WIM, 51.

60 Jan Patočka offers a similar reading of Heidegger's 'anxiety': 'In the slipping away of beings, which repel us and say nothing, the following becomes clear: only on the basis of something that is not a being could beings appear to us. [This is the] point of support around which a light, open region forms itself within which the appearing of beings is possible. This region is the *how and what* of beings that can address us; yet [this is] only present in refusing itself [...]. The region of the open, within which beings open up, is thus necessarily linked with

the self-withdrawal of being that intrudes in the form of the nothing'. Patočka, 'What Is Phenomenology?', 157–8.

61 Relatedly, see Heidegger's criticism against Daseinanalytic and the way Ludwig Binswanger applied Heidegger's ideas to psychiatry and psychotherapy. M. Heidegger, *Zollikon seminars: protocols, conversations, letters*, ed. M. Boss (Evanston, Illinois: Northwestern University Press, 2001), 193.

62 Ibid., 192–3.

63 As Heidegger puts it, commenting on Novalis: 'Philosophy can only be such an urge if we who philosophize are not at home everywhere. What is demanded by this urge? To be at home everywhere – what does that mean? Not merely here or there, nor even simply in every place, in all places taken together one after the other. Rather, to be at home everywhere means to be at once and at all times within the whole. We name this 'within the whole' and its character of wholeness *the world*. We are, and to the extent that we are, we are always waiting for something. We are always called upon by something as a whole. This 'as a whole' is the world.' Heidegger, *The Fundamental Concepts of Metaphysics*, 5.

64 As David Krell poetically puts it in WIM, 44.

Chapter 3

1 S. Kierkegaard, *Philosophical Fragments*, ed. H. Hong (Princeton: Princeton University Press, 1985), 37.

2 Plato, *Phaedrus*, trans. Ch. Rowe (London: Penguin Books, 2005), 229d–230b, translation modified.

3 This is the reason why I think it would not do to identify the Typhonic with the Dionysian, the more primitive, sexual and violent, and the un-Typhonic with the Apollonian, the more rational element of the soul.

4 The idea that the human fate is at least to some extent situated outside the human is also an important theme in Sophocles and the

Sophoclean ode about the *deinon* of the human being in *Antigone*, which Heidegger translates as the 'uncanny' and connects to the unhomely, out-of-joint nature of the human: 'manifold is the uncanny yet nothing uncannier than man bestirs itself, rising up beyond him' (πολλὰ τὰ δεινὰ κοὐδὲν ἀνθρώπου δεινότερον πέλει). There is a certain tension between the human being and the site in which it dwells, a tension that Heidegger describes as having access to Being while being in the midst of beings. This tension deserves wonder and anxiety. Heidegger writes in relation to the Sophoclean *deinon* what, I think, can also apply to what Socrates expresses: 'The *deinon* is that terrible in the sense of the overwhelming sway, which induces panicked fear, true anxiety, as well as collected, inwardly reverberating, reticent awe. [...] Beings as a whole, as the sway, are the overwhelming, *deinon* in the first sentence. But humanity is *deinon*, first, inasmuch as it remains exposed to this overwhelming sway, because it essentially belongs to Being. However, humanity is also deinon because it is violence doing in the sense we have indicated. It gathers what holds sway and lets it enter into an openness. [...] Because it is doubly *deinon*, it is to deinotaton, the most violent: violence doing in the midst of the overwhelming.' M. Heidegger, *Introduction to Metaphysics* (New Haven and London: Yale University Press, 2014), 167. Heidegger translates *deinon* as uncanny, because 'we understand the uncanny as that which throws one out of the canny, that is, the homely, the accustomed, the current, the unendangered. The unhomely does not allow us to be at home. Therein lies the overwhelming.' Ibid., 168. For a careful and thoughtful discussion of this, see Withy, *Heidegger on Being Uncanny*, 102–48.

5   T. Sheehan, 'Dasein', in *A Companion to Heidegger*, ed. H. L. Dreyfus and M. A. Wrathall (Oxford: Blackwell Publishing, 2005), 204.

6   Heidegger, *Introduction to Metaphysics*, 174.

7   Kierkegaard, *The Concept of Anxiety*, 47. I come back to why Adam is important for Kierkegaard's approach on anxiety.

8   *Philosophical Fragments*, 74.

9   Because it cannot be derived from anything else, the 'moment' is described by Climacus as a paradox: 'If the moment is posited, the

paradox is there, for in its most abbreviated form the paradox can be called the moment.' Ibid., 51. I discuss the nature and challenge of the paradox in Chapter 5.

10 As David Kangas puts it: 'The instant [moment] is the name for a beginning that cannot be interiorized, appropriated, recollected, represented, or possessed. [… It is] the gift or birth of presence. An instant [moment] cannot claim to be. Of itself it is nothing, it is nowhere.' D. Kangas, *Kierkegaard's Instant: On Beginnings* (Bloomington: Indiana University Press, 2007), 4.

11 He presents wonder and anxiety as 'moments' in the *Philosophical Fragments* (as Johannes Climacus) (1985) and in *The Concept of Anxiety* (as Vigilius Haufniensis) (1980). Since the latter was meant as a companion piece to the former, the two works are interconnected. According to David Kangas, the concept of the moment finds its most mature exploration in these two works: '[T]he clarification of the instant [moment] reaches its pitch in 1844 with the dual publication of *Philosophical Fragments* and *The Concept of Anxiety*'. Ibid., 160.

12 The concept of the 'moment' has Pauline connotations of a fullness of time, cases where the eternal and the temporal meet: in the *Fragments*, Climacus defines the moment as a resolution from eternity fulfilled in time (*Philosophical Fragments*, 25), and in *The Concept of Anxiety* Haufniensis defines it as the point where and when time and eternity touch each other (*The Concept of Anxiety*, 89). By 'eternity' Kierkegaard does not mean the continuation of life after we die, or some metaphysical plane of timelessness, but rather the opening of presence, a manifestation of our being-possible.

13 Going back to Socrates and the 'intimated paradox of the understanding [that] react[ed] upon […] his self-knowledge' (*Philosophical Fragments*, 39), we can, for example, find such a case of 'moment' in the voice of his daemon that speaks to him from time to time – including in the *Phaedrus*. In the middle of the dialogue, after Socrates has made a case against being-in-love (eros), arguing that love's narrow and lowly interests impede us from attaining freedom or truth, he receives a 'sign' from his daemon, the conscience-like voice that speaks to him from time to time. His daemon holds him back and

suggests to him that what he has just said in favour of the non-lover was offensively untrue. Socrates then makes another speech in favour of divine madness (which also manifests itself in erotic love) as what can allow us to attain truth. Unhuman elements, such as the divine madness that Socrates ends up praising and his own daemon that guides him, are presented, in the dialogue, as crucial for the attainment of truth.

Kierkegaard thinks that we can already find a version of the 'moment' in the Greeks: the *Fragments* mentions Aristotle's 'ἀκίνητος πάντα κινεῖ' (unmoved, he moves all) as an example of a beginning that 'cannot be converted into a principle or serve as a foundation', Kangas, *Kierkegaard's Instant*, 160. Further, in *The Concept of Anxiety* we read that Plato was attempting to conceive and understand the 'moment' as non-being under the category of time and that 'what [Kierkegaard] call[s] the 'moment' Plato called τὸ ἐξαίφνης [the sudden]'. See Kierkegaard, *The Concept of Anxiety*, 82 and 88 respectively. But the ancient Greek version of the 'moment' is limited. This is because for Kierkegaard a full apprehension of the 'moment' requires the conceptual availability of Christ's incarnation. The reason why the conceptual availability of the incarnation is important is because it captures in a concrete way the idea that the eternal can appear within time, interrupt time, but also infuse it, as it were, with possibility. In the Christian tradition this also takes the form of 'grace', as something that appears to come from outside the world (cannot be derived from anything in it) but can transform one's world. As Vigilius Haufniensis puts it: '[the moment] is the first reflection of eternity in time, its first attempt, as it were, at stopping time. For this reason, Greek culture did not comprehend the 'moment', and even if it had comprehended the atom of eternity, it did not comprehend that it was the 'moment', did not define it with a forward direction but with a backward direction. Because for Greek culture the atom of eternity was essentially eternity, neither time nor eternity received what was properly its due'. Kierkegaard, *The Concept of Anxiety*, 88.

14 In *Being and Time*, Heidegger distinguishes 'being' from 'spirit'. Insofar as 'spirit' comes from a Christian, onto-theological framework, it 'stands in the way of the basic question of *Dasein*'s Being (or leads it

off the track)'. B&T, 74, 48. Later in the text (without directly referring to Kierkegaard) he speaks against the centrality of 'spirit': 'man's "substance" is not spirit as a synthesis of soul and body; it is rather existence'. B&T, 153, 117. As I mentioned in Chapter 1, things are not as clear-cut as they may seem in the cited passage. Heidegger also works with theological concepts (such as 'falling', 'guilt', etc.) and it is never clear whether he manages to fully get rid of their theological weight. Further, it is not clear whether Kierkegaard's thinking can be reduced to an onto-theological position. As Clare Carlisle argues on the issue of spirit: 'From a Kierkegaardian point of view, it is difficult to maintain this distinction between spirit and existence. His account of spirit is thoroughly existential, and his account of existence is fundamentally spiritual. Throughout Kierkegaard's work we find an attempt to protect and preserve the spiritual meaning of human existence in a modern age that is characterized by "spiritlessness." This project reaches its clearest expression in *The Sickness unto Death* (1849), where Kierkegaard (writing under the pseudonym Anti-Climacus) states that spirit is at once our ontological constitution and our ethical task: we *are* spirit, but because we lose ourselves as spirit, we have the task of *becoming* spirit.' Carlisle, *A tale of two footnotes*, 39.

15 *The Concept of Anxiety*, 88.

16 Ibid., 43–4.

17 Ibid., 44.

18 As Reidar Thomte puts it: 'The psychology with which Kierkegaard worked [...] is a phenomenology that is based on an ontological view of man, the fundamental presupposition of which is the transcendent reality of the individual, whose intuitively discernible character reveals the existence of an eternal component. Such a psychology does not blend well with any purely empirical science and is best understood by regarding soma, psyche, and spirit as the principal determinants of the human structure, with the first two belonging to the temporal realm and the third to the eternal.' Thomte, R. 1980. 'Historical Introduction'. In Kierkegaard, *The Concept of Anxiety*, xiv.

19 As Haufniensis puts it: 'Let us now examine the narrative in Genesis more carefully as we attempt to dismiss the fixed idea that it is a myth, and as we remind ourselves that no age has been more skilful than our own in producing myths of the understanding, an age that produces myths and at the same time wants to eradicate all myths'. Kierkegaard, *The Concept of Anxiety*, 46.

20 Ibid., 47.

21 For a Heideggerian take on the myth of the Fall, see St. Mulhall, *Philosophical Myths of the Fall* (London and Princeton: Princeton University Press, 2005), 46–84.

22 *The Concept of Anxiety*, 25.

23 Ibid., 28.

24 Kierkegaard's interest in what he calls an adequate psychological account of anxiety is his way of breaking away from a theological tradition that places Adam in the realm of the fantastic and restricts anxiety and sin to Adam. As Lee Barrett puts it: 'The theological tradition had attempted to restrict this coinherence of the individual and the race to Adam alone. Vigilius Haufniensis, however, employs anxiety to show how the coinherence of the individual and the race can be regarded as a psychological phenomenon in everyone'. As Barrett further explains, Kierkegaard feared that the tradition had confused 'the descriptive generality of original sin (we are all sinners like Adam)' with some kind of 'causal necessity (we are all sinners because of what Adam did)'. See L. Barrett, 'Kierkegaard's "Anxiety" and the Augustinian Doctrine of Original Sin', in *International Kierkegaard Commentary, Volume 8: The Concept of Anxiety*, ed. R.L. Perkins. 35–62 (Macon, GA: Mercer University Press, 1985), 52 and 58.

25 S. Dunning, 'Kierkegaard's Systematic Analysis of Anxiety', in *International Kierkegaard Commentary, Volume 8: The Concept of Anxiety*, ed. R.L. Perkins. 7–34 (Macon, GA: Mercer University Press, 1985), 13.

26 Anxiety also plays such a structural role in Heidegger's work. As he remarks, the human existence is anxious in the very depths of its being. See B&T, 234, 190.

27 The term 'back' does not refer to a past event, but to our constitution (as expressed in a myth).

28 *The Concept of Anxiety*, 48.

29 Ibid., 44–5.

30 Ibid., 41.

31 Ibid., 45.

32 Ibid., 49.

33 Ibid., 41.

34 Ibid., 48.

35 Ibid., 53.

36 There is a tension in Kierkegaard's work between sin as an act and sin as a state, sin as something personal that one can be held responsible for versus sin as a suprapersonal state, prior to any personal decision. Barrett discusses this and explains the apparent tension by highlighting the idea that Kierkegaard deems it vital to investigate the human origin both in the context of dogmatics and in the context of psychology. Dogmatics offers the perspective on sin as state and psychology offers the perspective of sin as act: it is impossible to explain one through the other and vital that both figure in understanding the human existence; see Barrett, 'Kierkegaard's "Anxiety" and the Augustinian Doctrine of Original Sin'.

37 Kangas, *Kierkegaard's Instant: on Beginnings*, 161.

38 Barrett describes anxiety as an emotional episode and a pervasive potentiality: 'anxiety is not a mere emotional episode, but a pervasive potentiality. It is not a response to a particular object, but a response to all objects apprehended as possibilities for one's own free self-development. Consequently, Kierkegaard could describe anxiety as a state that endures before and after particular overt episodes'. See Barrett, 'Kierkegaard's "Anxiety" and the Augustinian Doctrine of Original Sin', 55. For a similar reading of a 'doubling' of anxiety in

Heidegger, namely the idea that it is ontic and ontological at the same time, see Withy, *Heidegger on Being Uncanny*.

39 Magurshak, 'The Concept of Anxiety: The Keystone of the Kierkegaard-Heidegger Relationship', 170.

40 'The actuality of the spirit constantly shows itself as a form that tempts its possibility but disappears as soon as it seeks to grasp for it, and it is a nothing that can only bring anxiety. More it cannot do as long as it merely shows itself.' Kierkegaard, *The Concept of Anxiety*, 42.

41 Magurshak, 'The Concept of Anxiety: The Keystone of the Kierkegaard-Heidegger Relationship', 173.

42 *The Concept of Anxiety*, 61.

43 Going back to Adam, the concept of the Fall may be relevant here but invites refinement and modification. Traditionally, we consider our fall as a *fait accompli* – the idea being that we have fallen out of Eden into our finite existence. But there is also a sense in which our state is the very movement of falling rather than a place where we have landed after our fall. The dizziness of anxiety when we experience it as individuals is a way in which we tune in to our fallenness/falling.

44 *The Concept of Anxiety*, 49.

Chapter 4

1 Such 'admiring wonder' comes with variations: our wonder at a skill or feature that we do not possess may or may not lead to an attempt to become or achieve what we admire. For example, in more profound versions of admiring wonder, like the case when we wonder at a hero or a god, we know that what deserves our wonder is essentially unknown or hard to achieve, and that we are excluded from what is wonderful about what we admire. Hannah Arendt makes this point, see H. Arendt, *The Life of the Mind* (New York: Harcourt, 1971), 142–3.

2 Heidegger, *Basic Questions of Philosophy*, 144.

3 'In this way, wonder now opens up what alone is wondrous in it: namely, the whole as the whole, the whole as beings, beings as a whole'. Ibid., 146.

4 Ibid., 144.

5 Ibid., 144–5.

6 'Origin' is the translation for the Greek αρχή (*arche*), which does not just mean 'beginning' in the temporal sense but also means a 'principle' or 'foundation'.

7 Aristotle's description of wonder is according to Arendt closer to wonder as aporia: '[…] it is because of wondering at things that humans, both now and at first, began to do philosophy. At the start, they wondered at those of the puzzles that where close to hand, then, advancing little by little, they puzzled over greater issues, for example, about the attributes of the moon and about issues concerning the sun and stars, and how the universe comes to be. Someone who puzzles or wonders, however, thinks himself ignorant (it is because of this indeed that the philosopher is in a way a mythlover, since myth is composed of wonders). So, if, indeed, it was because of [a desire] to avoid ignorance that they engaged in philosophy, it is evident that it was because of [a desire] to know that they pursued scientific knowledge, and not for the sake of some sort of utility'. Aristotle, *Metaphysics*, trans. C.D.C. Reeve (Indianapolis/Cambridge: Hackett Publishing, 2016), 982b.

8 Arendt, *The Life of the Mind*, 141.

9 T. Sheehan, 'What if Heidegger Were a Phenomenologist?', in *The Cambridge Companion to Heideggergist? if, indeed*, ed. M. Wrathall (Cambridge: Cambridge University Press, 2013), 381–401, 392.

10 Arendt, *The Life of the Mind*, 141.

11 Plato, *Theaetetus*, trans. John McDowell (Oxford: Oxford University Press, 2014), 146e, 10.

12 The Greek word for perception is αἴσθησις and the Greek work for appearing is φαίνεται. Hence, we read at 152 that φαντασία is the same as αἴσθησις.

13 Followed by two more versions of this: that a thing to which nothing is added and from which nothing is subtracted does not change but is always equal (ἴσον εἶναι), and that it is impossible that a thing should be (εἶναι) what it was not before, without having come to be (γενέσθαι) and coming to be (γίγνεσθαι). Notice the central role of 'being' in these remarks: to be, to have come to be, to be coming to be (becoming). I will come back to this later in the text.

14 For Plato, this wonder is a πάθος. The word πάθος is not easy to translate. It should be translated neither as 'experience' nor as 'feeling'. Instead, it is much closer to 'passion' and 'suffering', namely, it is a word that highlights the passivity of the wonderer. It is derived from the word πάσχειν ('to undergo', 'to suffer') – not in the all too ordinary sense of being in pain but in the sense that something happens *to* us, that we become subject to something – which is the etymological root of passivity. That this objectless wonder is a πάθος in the latter sense links back to Heidegger's point that, unlike other kinds of wonder, we cannot choose our way in or our way out, we are here more passive than in other ordinary cases.

15 Plato is not attempting to coin a new term with θαυμάζειν – the same word is used by Socrates when he sarcastically refers to his own amazement at Protagoras. Therefore, it is worthwhile to consider θαυμάζειν in conjunction with σκοτοδινιᾶν, a kind of dizziness associated with vertigo.

16 As Hannah Arendt also observes, 'Plato himself does not specify what his admiring wonder is directed at'. *The Life of the Mind*, 143.

17 See J. Rubenstein, *Strange Wonder: The Closure of Metaphysics and the Opening of Awe* (New York: Columbia University Press, 2008), 4.

18 Heidegger, *The Essence of Truth: On Plato's Cave Allegory and Theaetetus* (London: Bloomsbury, 2002).

19 I follow Heidegger's translation, which I think is the most faithful to
the text.

20 It is important that the series of 186, the part of the discussion on
colours, sounds and 'that it is' ends with going back to the original
question how it is possible that someone should attain the truth
(ἀλήθεια) if they don't attain being (οὐσία) and whether someone can
ever have knowledge of something whose truth they don't attain (see
186 c 7, 186 c 9). To these both Theaetetus replies 'no'. Thus, although
easy to miss when the dialogue is reduced to questions of epistemology
as *one* branch of philosophy, the theme of the dialogue (what is
knowledge) is very much connected to the question of what truth
is and what philosophy is; after all, the quest for what knowledge is was
first introduced in the dialogue as the question whether wisdom (that
which philosophy loves) is identical to knowledge. Furthermore, it is
important to note that no final definition of knowledge (and, therefore,
of the object of philosophy) is ever offered in the dialogue.

21 Arendt, *The Life of the Mind*, 144.

22 As Polt also remarks, even in those cases where there is no separate
word for 'being', the human being makes claims about things in a way
that presupposes a grasping of those things in their being: 'A Chinese
garment worker, in whose language subject and predicate can be
connected without a copula, still understands Being in every sentence
she uses, because her sentences are about entities, beings, things that
are. [...] Even when the Chinese woman is not speaking at all, but
just working at her sewing machine, she understands what it is for the
machine, the garments and herself to be. These entities, and countless
others, are available to her as entities, as things that matter to her, as
items that are meaningful and real in her world. [...] For her, as for all
of us, this understanding works perfectly well in the background of
everyday life – but it slips away as soon as we try to look at it head-on',
Heidegger: An Introduction, 27.

23 The Being of beings is, as Heidegger points out, the 'presence of what
is present'. See Heidegger, 'Introduction to "What Is Metaphysics?"', in
Pathmarks, ed. W. McNeill (Cambridge: Cambridge University Press,
1998), 277–90, 285–6.

24 Heidegger, quoted in Sheehan, 'What if Heidegger Were a Phenomenologist?', 383.

25 Sheehan, 'What if Heidegger Were a Phenomenologist?', 383.

26 Heidegger, *The Essence of Truth*, 127.

27 As Heidegger puts it: 'Everything is, after all, and nevertheless if we want to lay hold of being it is always as if we were reaching into a void. The being that we are asking about is almost like nothing, and yet we are always trying to arm and guard ourselves against the presumption of saying that all beings are not. But being remains undiscoverable, almost like nothing, or in the end entirely so. The word being is then finally just an empty word. It means nothing actual, tangible, real'. Heidegger, *Introduction to Metaphysics*, 39.

28 Heidegger, *The Fundamental Concepts of Metaphysics*, 180.

29 Heidegger, *Basic Questions of Philosophy*, 136.

30 See WIM, 57; *Introduction to Metaphysics*, 167; M. Heidegger, Postscript to 'What Is Metaphysics?' (1943), in *Pathmarks*, ed. W. McNeill (Cambridge: Cambridge University Press, 1998a), 231–8, 234.

31 For 'wonder' Kierkegaard uses the Danish 'Beundring' which is literally translated as 'admiration', but both his direct references to Plato and Aristotle (thaumazein) and the influence of the double meaning of the Latin 'admiratio' make it clear that in both texts I draw from, the *Philosophical Fragments* and *The Concept of Anxiety*, what he means by 'Beundring' is 'wonder'. For a more detailed commentary on this, see note 35 in *Philosophical Fragments*, 310.

32 See Rubenstein, *Strange Wonder*, 9.

33 In fact, in his own work Heidegger understands these two affective qualities of terror (*Erschrecken*) and awe (*Scheu*) as two compounds of another version of these fundamental dispositions, that of *Verhaltenheit* (reservedness or restraint) – although he never offers an extensive discussion of *Verhaltenheit*. But instead of seeing *Verhaltenheit* as an entirely different attunement, I think we should see it as what brings out the joint character of awe and horror. These elements of awe and horror are jointly present in such encounters with nothing as a response to the dual character of the encounter, namely, that in it we encounter simultaneously nothing and being: 'the nothing as that which is never and nowhere a being unveils itself as that which distinguishes itself from all beings, as that which we call being'. Heidegger, *Introduction to Metaphysics*, 233.

34 Although both Heidegger and Kierkegaard refer to wonder as a kind of suffering or distress (see Heidegger, *Basic Questions of Philosophy*, 133–5; Kierkegaard, *Philosophical Fragments*, 49–50), there are more frequent and direct mentions to the need to find wonder in anxiety rather than the other way around. Even when Heidegger speaks of the disposition of restraint, which I take to be a combination of a kind of wonder and anxiety (see previous footnote) – what he calls awe and terror – it is through awe that terror is sustained rather than the other way around. Although this is not an argument against their proximity, I take this to show the priority that presence (that things *are*) has over absence (the nothing, or that things are not). 'Nothing' is a facet of the 'givenness of meaning' rather than the other way around. Kierkegaard may be also alluding to this when, in response to those who reduce wonder to 'doubt', he speaks of the 'fundamental error of recent philosophy, that it wants to begin with the negative instead of with the positive, which always is the first'. Instead, he thinks that Descartes is right when he thinks that of all the passions, wonder is the first, and the only one that does not have an opposite (see *The Concept of Anxiety*, 146).

35 WIM, 57.

36 There is a continuity in Heidegger's thinking about wonder and anxiety that is also evident from the timeline of the development of his thinking around the nothing and the question 'Why are there beings at all rather than nothing?'. To present this timeline briefly: Heidegger's 1929 lecture 'What is Metaphysics?' ends with this question. Six years later, the same question opens the lecture course he gave in 1935, 'Introduction to Metaphysics', in which he discusses the fundamental question of metaphysics as what resonates in despair (when the sense of things grows dark), in heartfelt joy (when it seems as if things surround us as if for the first time) and in boredom. In 1929, he arrives at the question of metaphysics mainly through his discussion of the mood of anxiety, although other dispositions or attunements are also mentioned: boredom and joy in the presence of the *Dasein* of someone we love. In his 1929–30 lecture course, 'The Fundamental Concepts of Metaphysics', he offers an extensive discussion of the attunement of profound boredom as a way into the question of Being. Wonder is indirectly discussed in his lecture on the *Theaetetus* (1931–2) and directly in the Freiburg lectures (1937–8). This shows how these different attunements are simultaneously present in his thinking and inextricable from the emergence of philosophy/metaphysics.

37 αὐτουργός τῆς φιλοσοφίας. See *The Concept of Anxiety*, 162.

38 Heidegger formulates this question as 'Why are there beings at all, rather than nothing?'. See *Basic Questions of Philosophy*, 146–8; *Introduction to Metaphysics*, 2; WIM, 57.

39 Plato, *Phaedrus*, 279a, in WIM, 57.

40 WIM, 57.

41 The role and presence of these moods are not ahistorical. Heidegger thinks that, as a mood, wonder was more fitting to the ancient Greek times (see *Basic Questions of Philosophy*, 159), whereas boredom or anxiety may be closer to the world of today.

42 Think of when, in the *Meditations*, Descartes looks at the piece of wax and realizes how fleeting are the properties that are brought to his notice by the senses. Descartes's challenge is how to secure a ground, in his case *substance*, that allows for the wax to remain when all else is destroyed: 'But [...] while I am speaking, [the piece of wax] is brought close to the fire. The remains of its flavour evaporate; the smell fades; the colour is changed, the shape is taken away, it grows in size, becomes liquid, becomes warm, it can hardly be touched, and now, if you strike it, it will give off no sound. Does the same wax still remain? We must admit it does remain: no one would say or think it does not. So what was there in it that was so distinctly grasped? Certainly, none of those qualities I apprehended by the senses: for whatever came under taste, or smell, or sight, or touch, or hearing, has now changed: but the wax remains.' R. Descartes, *Meditations on*

First Philosophy, trans. M. Moriarty (Oxford: Oxford University Press, 2008), 22.

43 See Heidegger, *Basic Questions of Philosophy*, 150–1.

44 *Heidegger: An Introduction*, 2.

45 Withy, *Heidegger on Being Uncanny*, 75.

46 On the contrary, if the 'why' is understood as an investigation for a cause, as in Leibniz's case, it inevitably directs our attention toward entities. While the answers to this 'why' can vary – from the Big Bang to God as the first cause – viewing the 'why' as a search for a cause implies searching for another entity, even if it is a super-entity. However, in Heidegger's formulation of 'wonder', the perspective of entities that characterizes our usual and habitual engagement with the world becomes suspended. In the following passage, Heidegger clarifies that the question of metaphysics is a case of pure acknowledgment: 'While man is displaced [in wonder and the question], he himself is transformed into one who […] has to hold fast to beings as beings in pure acknowledgement. […] To sustain the basic disposition means to carry out the necessity of such questioning. Heidegger also speaks of a tolerating and "sustaining of the unexplainable"'. *Basic Questions of Philosophy*, 150–1 and 149 respectively. Heidegger is aware of the misconceptions that the link to Leibniz and the use of the 'Why' may cause: 'How can an attentive reader help feeling on the tip of his tongue an objection that is far more weighty than all protests against anxiety and the Nothing? The final question provokes the objection that a meditation that attempts to recall Being by way of the Nothing returns in the end to a question concerning beings. On top of that, the question even proceeds in the customary manner of metaphysics by beginning with a causal 'Why?' To this extent, then, the attempt to recall Being is fully repudiated in favour of a representational knowledge of beings in terms of beings. And to make matters still worse, the final question is obviously the question that the metaphysician Leibniz posed in his Principes de la nature et de la grâce.: 'Pourquoi y a-t-il quelque chose plutôt que rien ?'. *Introduction to 'What is Metaphysics?'*, 289.

Chapter 5

1 'Nothing' is a concept that leads to paradoxes, with the most famous
philosophical paradox being 'nothing comes from nothing', in Latin '*ex
nihilo nihil fit*' and in Greek 'οὐδὲν ἐξ οὐδενός'.

2 Some paradoxes that have led to philosophical problems have been
seen as solvable through the right distinctions. An example is Frege's
'the concept horse is not a concept', which can be resolved through
Wittgenstein's distinction between formal properties and material
properties. As he discusses in the *Tractatus Logico-Philosophicus* about
the concept of an 'object', the question 'What is an object?' can appear
as a baffling riddle, until we clarify that objects are not the kinds
of things that can be found in the world as a group of particulars,
like books, pens and flowers. See L. Wittgenstein, *Tractatus Logico-
Philosophicus*, trans. D.F. Pears and B.F. McGuinness (London:
Routledge, 1974), §4.1272.

3 In the literature on Kierkegaard, this problem has found expression
in a debate about whether the absolute paradox is against or above
reason. Evans (who treats the paradox mainly in response to the
Incarnation rather than, more generally, the relation between
possibility and actuality) summarizes his view as follows: 'So is the
paradox above reason or against reason? In a sense it is both. It is
above reason in that finite human beings cannot understand how God
could become a human person. It is against reason in that our concrete
human thinking, permeated by our sense of what is likely and unlikely,
which is in turn shaped by our own selfishness and experience of
others' selfishness, judges the possibility as the "strangest of all things."
However, it is not against reason in the sense of being against the laws
of logic. Or at least that is what the believer thinks. For one cannot
think that what has actually occurred is impossible, and the believer
believes in the reality of the God-man'. See D. Evans, *Passionate Reason:
Making Sense of Kierkegaard's Philosophical Fragments* (Bloomington:
Indiana University Press, 1992), 117. What this summary misses is
the priority of an attunement, a dimension that is also central for

faith, which, as Evans himself acknowledges, is a passion. As I discuss in this chapter, the paradox does not arise in reflection after the fact, but it is experienced in the dizziness of the anxious wonder and its 'psychological ambiguity' (Kierkegaard, *Philosophical Fragments*, 43). The question of the expression of that paradox and its clash with the rule of logic and reason comes after the fact.

4   R. Carnap, 'The Elimination of Metaphysics through the Logical Analysis of Language', in *Logical Positivism*, ed. A.J. Ayer (Glencoe, IL: The Free Press, 1959), 60–81.

5   For an extensive discussion of Wittgenstein's attitude to the issue of nonsense in relation to such experiences, see M. Balaska, *Wittgenstein and Lacan at the limit: Meaning and Astonishment* (London & New York: Palgrave Macmillan, 2019), and M. Balaska, 'Wittgenstein on Heidegger on the nothing', in *Early Analytic Philosophy: Origins and Transformations*, ed. J. Conant and G. Nir (London: Routledge, Forthcoming).

6   He writes: I can very well think what Heidegger meant about Being and Angst. Man has the drive to run up against the limits of language. Think, for instance, of the astonishment that anything exists. *This astonishment cannot be expressed in the form of a question*, and there is also no answer to it. All that we can say can only, *a priori*, be nonsense. Nevertheless we run up against the limits of language. Kierkegaard also saw this running-up and similarly pointed it out (as running up against paradox). […] the tendency to run up against *shows something*. The holy Augustine already knew this when he said: 'What, you swine, you would speak no nonsense? Go ahead and speak nonsense – it doesn't matter!' L. Wittgenstein, *Ludwig Wittgenstein and the Vienna Circle: Conversations Recorded by Friedrich Waismann*, ed. B. McGuinness, trans. B. McGuinness and J. Schulte (New York: Barnes and Noble Books, 1979), 68–9, translation modified.

7   L. Wittgenstein, 'A Lecture on Ethics', in *Philosophical Occasions* 1912–1951, ed. J. Klagge and A. Nordmann (Indianapolis & Cambridge: Hackett Publishing Company, 1993), 37–44, 41–2, my emphasis.

8   Ibid., 42.

9 Ibid., 43–4.

10 See *Tractatus Logico-Philosophicus*, §6.44. In §5.552 of the *Tractatus*, Wittgenstein provides another brief remark on the dimension of 'that it is', linking it also to intelligibility, to the condition for understanding logic.

> 'The "experience" that we need to understand logic is not that something or other is the state of things, but that something is; that, however, is not an experience.
> Logic is prior to every experience – that something is so.
> It is prior to the How, not prior to the What'.

Understanding the background of intelligibility and sense-making, is based on a strange kind of experience. Wittgenstein's scepticism of the term 'experience' may not greatly differ from Heidegger's reasons for distancing his descriptions of moods from conventional psychological accounts of experiences. Treating 'that something is' as the object of an experience may result in conflating 'that something is' with 'how things are'. In Heideggerian terms, we might refer to this as a confusion between the ontic and the ontological. Yet, Wittgenstein does not entirely abandon the term 'experience'; he uses the word, albeit with quotation marks around it. In §6.45 he associates this dimension with what he calls the mystical, a way of feeling the world as a limited whole.

11 Wittgenstein, 'A Lecture on Ethics', 44.

12 In 'What Is Metaphysics?' Heidegger writes that his expressions violate the rule of 'logic' (48), using inverted commas around the word, which Carnap never addresses.

13 This comes up when Carnap criticizes metaphysical statements as pseudo-statements (*Scheinsätze*): 'The metaphysician believes that he travels in territory in which truth and falsehood are at stake. In reality, however, he has not asserted anything, but only expressed something, like an artist'. Carnap, 'The Elimination of Metaphysics through the Logical Analysis of Language', 76.

14 A similar psychological diagnosis of confusion takes place from the perspective of the later Wittgenstein when Gordon Baker treats Heidegger's choice to make certain claims about 'nothing' as a case of being under the grip of an illusion, a picture that holds him captive. See G. Baker, 'Wittgenstein's Method and Psychoanalysis', in *Wittgenstein's Method: Neglected Aspects. Essays on Wittgenstein by Gordon Baker*, ed. K. Morris (Oxford: Blackwell, 2004). Sadly, the rejection of metaphysical concepts does not only result from seeing language's function as the representation of facts which is sometimes (wrongly) considered as an early Wittgenstein view, but also from those readings of Wittgenstein's later work as prioritizing the everyday and opposing concepts such as 'being', 'language' and 'nothing'. For an extended critical discussion of Baker's remarks and an analysis of where they go wrong, see Balaska, 'Wittgenstein on Heidegger on the nothing'.

15 WIM, 48.

16 As Heidegger writes: 'To be sure, man's prescientific and extra-scientific activities also are related to beings. But science is exceptional in that, in a way peculiar to it, it gives the matter itself explicitly and solely the first and last word. In such impartiality of inquiring, determining, and grounding, a peculiarly delineated submission to beings themselves obtains, in order that they may reveal themselves.' WIM, 46.

17 Mapping logic and language on science finds its fullest historical expression in what was called logical positivism – a term that combines logic with science. Wittgenstein's distance from logical positivism is expressed in the fact that he raises similar concerns about science in 'A Lecture on Ethics' when he juxtaposes seeing something as a fact with seeing something as a miracle: 'the scientific way of looking at a fact is not the way to look at it as a miracle.' See Wittgenstein, 'A Lecture on Ethics', 43.

18 WIM, 47.

19 Ibid., 46.

20 Relatedly, Patočka calls philosophy 'a science of nothing', to emphasize that its object is not any entity within the world, but the fact that things are and that we are at all. As he writes: 'For this reason, [philosophy] can also be called, albeit paradoxically, a science *of nothing*. For the object of philosophy *is* indeed nothing of which one can say "it is" or "there is" this object; rather, the object of philosophy is this "there is" itself'. See Patočka, 'What is Phenomenology?', 152.

21 L. Wittgenstein, *Philosophical Investigations*, trans. G.E.M. Anscombe, P.M.S. Hacker and J. Schulte (Oxford: Wiley-Blackwell, 2009), §23.

22 Kierkegaard, *Philosophical Fragments*, 50.

23 Ibid., 52.

24 Heidegger discusses this priority of attunement over cognition in *Being and Time*. We cannot know why the world as a whole (nothing) weighs down on us: '*Dasein* cannot know anything of the sort because the possibilities of disclosure which belong to cognition reach far too short a way compared with the primordial disclosure belonging to moods, in which *Dasein* is brought before its Being as "there". B&T, 173, 135.

Chapter 6

1 There is nothing wrong with making use of public interpretations apart from the fact that they can obscure our openness and turn our human existence into a given rather than a question or a task. When we rely too much on preconceived schemas and interpretations, our understanding of ourselves and other entities is 'taken up by, what is typically said about them – how they are to be understood, how anyone and everyone understands them'. This can result in 'a peculiarly unquestioning relation to all the beings we encounter in our world'. Mulhall, *Philosophical Myths of the Fall*, 51.

2 In his discussion of experiences, like wonder, that open us onto what he calls 'the spiritual life', Patočka brings in a famous fragment by Heraclitus, 'The thunderbolt steers all things', as an analogy for the double aspect of what takes place: 'the flash [...] reveals the light of dawn in darkness but at the same time [it] reveals the darkness', namely it reveals our openness and at the same time our open-endedness (finitude). J. Patočka, 'The Spiritual Person and the Intellectual', in *Care for the Soul: The Selected Writings of Jan Patočka*, ed. I. Chvatic and E. Plunkett (London: Bloomsbury, 2022), 294–305, 299–300.

3   Sheehan, 'Dasein', 205.

4   Patočka, 'The Spiritual Person and the Intellectual', 296.

5   L. Wittgenstein, *Zettel* (Oxford: Blackwell Publishing, 1988), §456.

6   Patočka, 'The Spiritual Person and the Intellectual', 299.

7   In Heideggerian terms this means to be open to the ontological difference. As discussed earlier the question 'Why are there beings, rather than nothing?', a question that emerges from wonder and anxiety, allows for a cultivation of philosophy, for becoming, as Kierkegaard puts it, 'αὐτουργός τῆς φιλοσοφίας'.

8   Patočka, 'The Spiritual Person and the Intellectual', 298. The difficulty in offering defining traits of the spiritual person's life is so characteristic of it that Patočka turns it into its defining trait. Whereas 'the cultural person is something self-evident; they perform certain activities that can be externally stated, described, and defined -sociologically, economically, etc-', the spiritual person 'is a horrible problem'. Ibid., 296. Wittgenstein also remarks on the difficulty of pointing to specific facts that distinguish a life that feels the world as a limited whole or views the world *sub specie aeterni*. This dimension, *that* things are, is something that can be made manifest but cannot be exhaustively described in propositional facts. See Wittgenstein, *Tractatus Logico-Philosophicus*, §6.44; §6.45; §6.522.

9   'Dasein is an entity for which, in its Being, that Being is an issue.' B&T, 236, 191.

10 Kierkegaard, *The Concept of Anxiety*, 157.

11 One may want to object that this begins to resemble a chicken-egg problem, for it seems that to be ready for anxiety and wonder, we need to be able to recognize what anxiety and wonder are meant to be teaching us in the first place. To respond to this, we should keep in mind that both anxiety and wonder were discussed as attunements that

interrupt our ordinary mode of being-in-the-world, in other words, they are both sudden and unexpected. Preparation does not remove that sudden character. But on the other hand, a life closed to their insights makes it harder to feel the power of these attunements.

12 Kierkegaard, *The Concept of Anxiety*, 155.

13 Heidegger, *Basic Questions of Philosophy*, 154.

14 Ibid., 147. In the same text, Heidegger offers a description of the preparation for wonder in terms of a carrying out of τέχνη, a way of bringing φύσις into unconcealment. For more, see ibid., 151–5.

15 Kierkegaard, *The Concept of Anxiety*, 157.

16 Ibid., 144.

17 B&T, 232, 188.

18 Kierkegaard, *The Concept of Anxiety*, 156.

19 M. Heidegger, 'Postscript to "What Is Metaphysics?"', 234.

20 This is to see 'the telling refusal of beings [*Versagen*]' as 'in itself a telling [*Sagen*], i.e., a making manifest of the as a whole', Heidegger, *The Fundamental Concepts of Metaphysics*, 141.

21 Heidegger, *Postscript to 'What Is Metaphysics?' (1943)*, 234.

22 Patočka, 'The Spiritual Person and the Intellectual', 296.

23 See Wittgenstein, *Tractatus Logico-Philosophicus*, §6.43.

24 Heidegger, *Postscript to 'What Is Metaphysics?' (1943)*, 236.

BIBLIOGRAPHY

Adorno, T.W. *The Jargon of Authenticity*, trans. K. Tarnowski and F. Will. Evanston, IL: Northwestern University Press, 1973.

American Psychiatric Association. *American Psychiatric Association: Diagnostic and Statistical Manual of Mental Disorders*. Fifth Edition. Arlington, VA: American Psychiatric Association, 2013.

Arbiser, S. 'An Unexpected Clinical Experience: Rethinking Affects'. In *On Freud's 'Inhibitions, Symptoms and Anxiety'*, ed. S. Arbiser and J. Schneider, 415–35. London: Karnac Books, 2013.

Arendt, H. *The Life of the Mind*. New York: Harcourt, 1971.

Aristotle. *Metaphysics*, trans. C.D.C. Reeve. Indianapolis and Cambridge: Hackett Publishing, 2016.

Baker, G. 'Wittgenstein's Method and Psychoanalysis'. In *Wittgenstein's Method: Neglected Aspects. Essays on Wittgenstein by Gordon Baker*, ed. K. Morris, 205–222. Oxford: Blackwell, 2004.

Balaska, M. *Wittgenstein and Lacan at the limit: Meaning and Astonishment*. London and New York: Palgrave Macmillan, 2019.

Balaska, M. 'Wittgenstein on Heidegger on the nothing'. In *Early Analytic Philosophy: Origins and Transformations*, ed. J. Conant and G. Nir. London: Routledge, Forthcoming.

Barrett, L. 'Kierkegaard's "Anxiety" and the Augustinian Doctrine of Original Sin'. In *International Kierkegaard Commentary, Volume 8: The Concept of Anxiety*, ed. R.L. Perkins, 35–62. Macon, GA: Mercer University Press, 1985.

Blattner, W.D. *Heidegger's Being and Time: A Reader's Guide*. New York: Continuum, 2006.

Carlisle, C. 'A Tale of Two Footnotes: Heidegger and the Question of Kierkegaard'. In *Heidegger, Authenticity, and the Self: Themes from Division Two of Being and Time*, ed. D. McManus, 37–55. London: Routledge, 2015.

Carnap, R. 'The Elimination of Metaphysics through the Logical Analysis of Language'. In *Logical Positivism*, ed. A.J. Ayer, 60–81. Glencoe, IL: The Free Press, 1959.

Descartes, R. *Meditations on First Philosophy*, trans. M. Moriarty. Oxford: Oxford University Press, 2008.

Dreyfus, H.L. *Being-in-the-World: A Commentary on Heidegger's Being and Time, Division I*. Cambridge, MA: The MIT Press, 1991.

Dunning, S. 'Kierkegaard's Systematic Analysis of Anxiety'. In *International Kierkegaard Commentary, Volume 8: The Concept of Anxiety*, ed. R.L. Perkins, 7–34. Macon, GA: Mercer University Press, 1985.

Dupré, L. 'Of Time and Eternity'. In *International Kierkegaard Commentary, Volume 8: The Concept of Anxiety*, ed. R.L. Perkins, 111–32. Macon, GA: Mercer University Press, 1985.

Evans, D. *Passionate Reason: Making Sense of Kierkegaard's*. Philosophical Fragments. Bloomington: Indiana University Press, 1992.

Freud, S. *Studies on Hysteria*. SE 2. London: Hogarth Press, 1893–1895 (Standard Edition is abbreviated as SE).

Freud, S. *Introductory Lectures on Psycho-Analysis*. SE 16, 15–16. London: Hogarth Press, 1916–1917.

Freud, S. 'The Uncanny'. In *An Infantile Neurosis and Other Works*, SE 17. London: Hogarth Press, 1917–1919.

Freud, S. *Inhibitions, Symptoms and Anxiety*. SE 20. London: Hogarth Press, 1925–1926.

Glas, G. 'Anxiety-Animal Reactions and the Embodiment of Meaning'. In *Nature and Narrative: An Introduction to the New Philosophy of Psychiatry*, ed. B. Fulford, K. Morris, J. Sadler and G. Stanghellini, 231–49. Oxford: Oxford University Press, 2003.

Glas, G. 'An Enactive Approach to Anxiety and Anxiety Disorders'. *Philosophy, Psychiatry, & Psychology* 27, no. 1 (2020): 35–50.

Harari, R. *Lacan's Seminar on 'Anxiety': An Introduction*. New York: Other Press, 2001.

Heidegger, M. *Being and Time*, trans. J. Macquarrie and E. Robinson. New York: Harper & Row, 1962 (*Being and Time* is abbreviated as B&T).

Heidegger, M. *Basic Questions of Philosophy: Selected 'Problems' of 'Logic'*. Bloomington: Indiana University Press, 1994.

Heidegger, M. *The Fundamental Concepts of Metaphysics: World, Finitude, Solitude*. Bloomington: Indiana University Press, 1995.

Heidegger, M. *Pathmarks*. Cambridge: Cambridge University Press, 1998a.

Heidegger, M. 'Introduction to "What Is Metaphysics?"'. In *Pathmarks*, ed. W. McNeill, 277–90. Cambridge: Cambridge University Press, 1998b.

Heidegger, M. 'Postscript to "What Is Metaphysics?" (1943)'. In *Pathmarks*, ed. W. McNeill, 231–8. Cambridge: Cambridge University Press, 1998c.

Heidegger, M. *Zollikon Seminars: Protocols, Conversations, Letters*, ed. M. Boss. Evanston, IL: Northwestern University Press, 2001.

Heidegger, M. *The Essence of Truth: On Plato's Cave Allegory and Theaetetus*. London: Bloomsbury, 2002.

Heidegger, M. 'What Is Metaphysics?'. In *Basic Writings*, ed. and trans. D.F. Krell, 41–57. London: Routledge, 2011 ('What Is Metaphysics?' is abbreviated as WIM).

Heidegger, M. *Introduction to Metaphysics*. New Haven and London: Yale University Press, 2014.

Heidegger, M. *Logic: The Question of Truth* (Studies in Continental Thought), trans. T. Sheehan. Bloomington: Indiana University Press, 2016.

Hoffmann, E.T.A. 'The Sandman'. In *The Golden Pot and Other Tales*, trans. Ritchie Robertson. Oxford: Oxford University Press, 1992.

Jentsch, E. 'On the Psychology of the Uncanny'. *Angelaki: A New Journal in Philosophy, Literature and the Social Sciences* 2, no. 1 (1996): 7–16.

Kangas, D. *Kierkegaard's Instant: On Beginnings*. Bloomington: Indiana University Press, 2007.

Kierkegaard, S. *The Concept of Anxiety*, ed. and trans. R. Thomte and A.B. Anderson. Princeton: Princeton University Press, 1980.

Kierkegaard, S. *Philosophical Fragments*, trans. H.V. Hong and E.H. Hong. Princeton: Princeton University Press, 1985.

Lacan, J. *Anxiety. The Seminar: Book 10*, trans. A.R. Price, ed. J.-A. Miller. Cambridge: Polity Press, 2014.

Levinas, E. *On Escape*, trans. B. Bergo. Stanford, CA: Stanford University Press, 2003.

Magurshak, D. 'The Concept of Anxiety: The Keystone of the Kierkegaard-Heidegger Relationship'. In *International Kierkegaard Commentary, Volume 8: The Concept of Anxiety*, ed. R.L. Perkins, 167–95. Macon, GA: Mercer University Press, 1985.

Masschelein, A. 2012. *The Unconcept: The Freudian Uncanny in Late-Twentieth-Century Theory*. Albany: SUNY Press.

Mawson, C. *Psychoanalysis and Anxiety: From Knowing to Being*. London: Routledge, 2019.

McManus, D. 'Anxiety, Choice, and Responsibility'. In *Heidegger, Authenticity and the Self: Themes from Division Two of Being and Time*, ed. D. McManus, 163–85. London: Routledge, 2015.

Mulhall, St. *Philosophical Myths of the Fall*. London and Princeton: Princeton University Press, 2005.

Patočka, J. 'The Spiritual Person and the Intellectual'. In *Care for the Soul: The Selected Writings of Jan Patočka*, ed. I. Chvatic and E. Plunkett, 294–305. London: Bloomsbury, 2022a.

Patočka, J. 'What Is Phenomenology?'. In *Care for the Soul: The Selected Writings of Jan Patočka*, ed. I. Chvatic and E. Plunkett, 139–62. London: Bloomsbury, 2022b.

Philipse, H. *Heidegger's Philosophy of Being*. Princeton: Princeton University Press, 1998.

Plato. *Phaedrus*, trans. Ch. Rowe. London: Penguin Books, 2005.

Plato. *Theaetetus*, trans. J. McDowell. Oxford: Oxford University Press, 2014.

Polt, R. *Heidegger: An Introduction*. Ithaca, NY: Cornell University Press, 1999.

Ratcliffe, M. 'Why Mood Matters'. In *The Cambridge Companion to Heidegger's Being and Time*, ed. M. Wrathall, 157–76. Cambridge: Cambridge University Press, 2013.

Rubenstein, J. *Strange Wonder: The Closure of Metaphysics and the Opening of Awe*. New York: Columbia University Press, 2008.

Sartre, J.-P. *Nausea*. London: Penguin Books, 1963.

Sheehan, T. 'Heidegger's "Introduction to the Phenomenology of Religion, 1920–21"'. In *A Companion to Martin Heidegger's Being and Time*, ed. J.J. Kockelmans, 40–62. Washington, DC: Center for Advanced Research in Phenomenology & University Press of America, 1986.

Sheehan, T. 'Dasein'. In *A Companion to Heidegger*, ed. H. L. Dreyfus and M. A. Wrathall, 193–213. Oxford: Blackwell Publishing, 2005.

Sheehan, T. 'What if Heidegger Were a Phenomenologist?'. In *The Cambridge Companion to Heidegger's Being and Time*, ed. M. Wrathall, 381–401. Cambridge: Cambridge University Press, 2013.

Staehler, T. 'How Is a Phenomenology of Fundamental Moods Possible?'. *International Journal of Philosophical Studies* 15, no. 3 (2007): 415–33.

Thomte, R. 'Historical Introduction'. In *The Concept of Anxiety*, ed. S. Kierkegaard, vii–xviii. Princeton: Princeton University Press, 1980.

Withy, K. *Heidegger on Being Uncanny*. Cambridge, MA: Harvard University Press, 2015.

Wittgenstein, L. *Tractatus Logico-Philosophicus*, trans. D.F. Pears and B.F. McGuinness. London: Routledge, 1974.

Wittgenstein, L. *Ludwig Wittgenstein and the Vienna Circle: Conversations Recorded by Friedrich Waismann*, ed. B. McGuinness, trans. B. McGuinness and J. Schulte. New York: Barnes and Noble Books, 1979.

Wittgenstein, L. *Zettel*. Oxford: Blackwell Publishing, 1988.

Wittgenstein, L. 'A Lecture on Ethics'. In *Philosophical Occasions 1912–1951*, ed. J. Klagge and A. Nordmann, 37–44. Indianapolis and Cambridge: Hackett Publishing, 1993.

Wittgenstein, L. *Philosophical Investigations*, trans. G.E.M. Anscombe, P.M.S. Hacker and J. Schulte. Oxford: Wiley-Blackwell, 2009.

INDEX